THE FEASTS OF MEMORY

Stories of a Greek Family

THE FEASTS OF MEMORY

ISLAND OF KASOS

Stories of a Greek Family

BY ELIAS KULUKUNDIS

PETER E. RANDALL PUBLISHER
PORTSMOUTH, NEW HAMPSHIRE
2003

The Feasts of Memory has been revised by the author
especially for this edition and includes a new chapter,
"Vacations Afloat," about the transition from sail to
steam on board his grandfather's ships.

ISBN 1-931807-11-6

Library of Congress Control Number: 2002095903

Peter E. Randall Publisher
P.O. Box 4724
Portsmouth, NH 03801
www.perpublisher.com

Book design: Grace Peirce

Watercolor on front cover by Manuel Kulukundis

For my daughter Delia

CONTENTS

Preface

When I first published The Feasts of Memory, people used to ask me, "Is it a novel? A travel book? An autobiography?"

In *American Literary History* ("The Other Space of Greek America," Winter 1998), Professor Yiorgios Kalogeras wrote that the book "stands out as an autobiography, a family memoir, a history and cartography of the island of Kasos, a book of short stories, and a travel narrative all in one."

That settles the question. The answer is all of the above.

Recently, I heard that my young nephew gave the book to his fiancée as an engagement present, presumably because he wanted to let her know his origins.

"This is our book," he said.

The gesture filled me with satisfaction and gratitude. When I wrote the book at age twenty-eight, I was concerned only with understanding my life. Now, the passage of time and the advent of another generation has given the book a dimension I did not anticipate.

For this edition, I have tried to revise and update the text to improve the experience for the reader without changing the essential nature of the original. That has involved cutting out a few anachronisms and obvious excesses, while at the same time leaving the whole intact and rendering it clearer and more accessible to the general reader.

I have added a chapter entitled "Vacations Afloat"

which contains new material about my grandfather's successful navigation from the age of sail to the age of steam, and I have included a portrait of my uncle Manuel Kulukundis who was perhaps overshadowed in the first edition by his elder brother George.

ACKNOWLEDGMENTS

*I*n writing *The Feasts of Memory,* I acknowledge my debt to the following sources:

History of the Greek Revolution by Thomas Gordon.

History of Greece by George Finlay.

History of Kasos by T. Evangelides and M. Michailides-Nouaros.

The Island of Roses and her Eleven Sisters by Michael Volonakis.

Italy's Aegean Possessions by Booth and Booth.

The files of *The Dodecanesian,* published by the Dodecanesian League of America and the Dodecanesian National Council.

"Vacations Afloat" by Manuel E. Kulukundis.

Modern Greek Folklore and Ancient Greek Religion, by John Cuthbert Lawson.

Legal Customs of the Dodecanese by M. Michailides-Nouaros.

Kasiotika, a collection of Kasiot lore by Reverend Zacharias Halkiades. (I am indebted to the author for personally answering my questions).

No one could write on Kasos and Dodecanese without drawing on the work of Dr. Nicholas Mavris, who after the Enosis of the Dodecanese with Greece became the first Governor General of Rhodes. I am indebted to his Historical Archive of Kasos,

Dodecanesian Library and Dodecanesian Lyre, a collection of songs and dances of the Dodecanese.

I remember with gratitude the many hours Dr. Mavris spent with me, his hospitality in throwing open his personal library and directing me to the sources I required, and the bright example of his scholarship. In addition, there were many aspects of Dr. Mavris' personality—combining his work as a doctor, a scholar, and finally as Governor of Rhodes—that I was too young to appreciate when he was living but remember with admiration now.

I cannot name all the Kasiots who shared their memories with me, but I am grateful to all of them.

I also appreciate the help of friends who read the manuscript and offered suggestions.

My special thanks to Peter Randall and his team for a happy publishing experience.

Aphrodite at the House of the Blue Shutters.

ARRIVAL

I did not see Kasos until I was twenty-seven, when I made this journey. I have never lived there, and neither have my parents. They were born on Syros, another island two hundred miles up the Aegean. I was born in London, came to America when I was three, and have lived here ever since.

Only my grandparents were native Kasiots, all four of them. My grandfathers were sea captains, and at the turn of the century they emigrated to Syros, then the largest port in Greece. After the First World War, they emigrated to a still larger port: London.

My father and his brothers took over the shipping business their father had begun. Eventually, in 1939, my parents extended the emigration farther to America. They settled in Rye, a suburb of New York, where I spent all but the first three years of childhood.

This journey will be back along the course of that emigration. The destination is Kasos, the final island. On the way back we come first to Syros, capital and metropolis of the Cyclades. Syros was where my parents met for the first time, when my father was six years old and my mother an infant.

1

It was at my mother's christening. My mother was in her godfather's arms; my father was standing beside his own mother, the youngest in a row of five brothers ranging in age from six to twenty. They met in a house filled with relatives and neighbors on a mountainside of scrubbed white houses, rising like an amphitheater before the ever various spectacle of the Aegean Sea. At the windows of that house, looking southward down the Archipelago, we are two hundred miles from Kasos and one generation still to go.

Syros, like London, was a way station in the journey. My grandparents lived there as immigrants, as almost everyone in Syros was at one time. Except for a few natives descended from medieval times, Syros was settled by people of other islands—Chios, Psara, Crete, and Kasos—all made homeless by the Greek Revolution against the Turks in the 1820s.

Much later, at the end of the nineteenth century, when my grandparents sailed to this first America, there was already a Kasiot quarter waiting for them, just as there were Chiot and Psariot quarters. As Kasiot children, my parents felt different from the other children of Syros, just as they were later to feel as adults in London, and their own children were to feel in Rye, New York.

But if my parents were not true natives of Syros, still it was their beginning. My mother's father built a villa in the hills, and my parents helped preserve it ever since his death and returned to it summer after summer. They kept it as a memorial to their parents and their childhood, a reminder of what they were before they embarked on outward voyages to begin their life together in an alien land, then raise their children in yet another one.

It is a familiar story in a Greek life. Exile is a Greek experience, and there is even a Greek word for it that does not exist in other languages. It is *xenitia,* which is not exactly exile because it can be self-imposed, and not estrangement because there is no spiritual estrangement. *Xenitia* is simply the loss of the native land. It is an old experience in the Greek mind, as old as the pre-Christian Greeks who spread from the native peninsula in an ever-widening diaspora to other shores of the Mediterranean, the Red Sea, and the Black.

Despite this sense of exile, which haunts him to the grave, the Greek is ever journeying, especially the islander, hemmed in only by the horizon. This Greek is arriving or departing, on the way out or on the way back. No sooner did my parents take the outward journey than the horizon opened toward their way home. No sooner did they cross a continent to Europe and an ocean to New York than they repeated the journey in the reverse direction, performing it in a continual celebration of the same event, a perennial round-trip of reconciliation and farewell.

But my journey back was different. I had no memory of Syros, no image of a native island, of a villa with a red gabled roof and groves of olive, orange, and lemon trees descending from it on orderly terraces of land. When I awoke to memory, Syros was beyond me.

The first place I remember is a room in a country club in Rye, New York, where my parents had come to live. That country club is a huge stone edifice erupting out of the suburban landscape, with statues and porticoes, vaults and gargoyles. To this day I wonder how my parents found it. To Greek immigrants it must have been the epitome of strangeness.

"Here is America," my father must have thought, as he settled down with his family in a cavernous fortress from "A Diamond as Big as the Ritz." Here, in this gigantic relic of a lost America, my Greek childhood began. Downstairs, in a vaulted dining room, my parents sat around an oval table with friends and relatives, most of them not only Greeks, but Kasiots. Meanwhile, upstairs, by windows that overlooked an outdoor dance floor and ultimately a golf course, I lay in bed, puzzling out the arabesques on my carpeted hotel floor.

After some months my parents bought a house nearby, and after a while I did not think to ask how we had arrived there. I did not think of journeys then, because for a child there are no arrivals and departures, no past and future, only *now*. It was years later when I saw Syros.

In the meantime, I had to understand as best I could that I lived in a Greek house in Rye, New York. It was a house in Rye where the Greek language was spoken, Greek food was on the table, and Greek people gathered in the evening after an hour's drive from New York City, sitting together in their *xenitia,* before a window that overlooked the golf course and the hills of Westchester County.

As for Greece, I knew nothing of it. As a nation it was slumbering in my mind, just as it had slumbered for centuries in the Ottoman Empire before awakening to discover itself in 1821. Through those years of darkness, the same agents worked on me as had worked on the medieval subjects of the sultan: parents, priests, and teachers. They taught me its language, religion, and history; but none of them succeeded in convincing me that it really existed anywhere.

The only Greece I could believe in was the Greece I knew. Greece was downstairs in our house in Rye, as I sat by the banister on the second floor, watching the people in our living room, listening to their babel of words and laughter.

Greece was downstairs on a Sunday night, while upstairs, in America, I answered questions in my workbook before going to bed. Greece was Monday and Thursday afternoons when a Greek teacher arrived on the train from New York City to teach me the pluperfect and future perfect of Greek verbs when elsewhere, in America, other children were playing baseball.

Greece was the church I went to, where there were icons with mournful faces. Greece was the nights when there were guests, familiar yet unrecognizable, speaking in obscure liquid syllables, when my mother served tiny balls, vine leaves with meat and rice inside, and a soup of egg and lemon that had a different taste a moment after you swallowed it.

Greece was afterward, when I lay in bed and heard the train of voices rumbling on beneath me: a low subterranean echo of another life.

It was not really Greece, only its echo sounding through corridors of war and emigration. I did not see the real Greece until I was seventeen, when I emerged from my tunnel of ignorance into the shining reality at its end, like the underground river that began in Hades and flowed out of the abode of darkness to the sea. That was in 1954, when after fourteen years of *xenitia,* my parents first returned to the island of their birth.

That summer, sailing southeast from Athens' port city, Piraeus, I saw the island of Syros. It lay horizontally before the ship, the prow intersecting it as though for landfall. However long we sailed toward it, we seemed to reach no closer. Hours it lay before us: receding, chimerical.

Finally, as we began to overtake it, we could make out only a spine of mountains, betraying no sign of life: a whitened skeleton, petrified with age. As we rounded the northeastern tip, the island began to recede again, hiding behind a rocky promontory. After so many hours, we were perilously close, across a hundred yards of bottomless blue water. And still there was no sign of life. Still the island could be an abandoned relic, picked clean by centuries of Aegean pirates.

Now, as the land loomed up suddenly beside us, there was a crowd at the rail. A hush had fallen on the ship and we heard each throb of the slackening engines as silently the land slipped by. Everyone was waiting, because a voyage has a natural drama of its own and the landfall is its climax.

We followed the scaly promontory, verging toward it so that it seemed eventually we must collide against its rocks. And behind it somewhere was the island, out of sight, elusive to the last. Still there was no sign of life. Still Syros was a heap of ash, reddened in the setting sun: a volcanic cinder in a timeless sea.

Then, at last it happened. I was standing with my father at the rail, and afterward he told me he had been expecting it. He remembered it from the countless landfalls of his childhood. But for me it was happening for the first time, and the first blast took me by surprise.

It was the ship's whistle sounding over that island of the dead like the last trumpet. The first few moments I saw and heard nothing, waiting for the blast to be over. But it wasn't. Long moments it sustained itself and grew louder: a chord struck on a maddened organ. Then it was silent.

Sight and sound returned to us assaulted passengers. And when I looked again at the island, a lonely chapel had appeared on a cliff above the ship, as though summoned to existence by the whistle itself. In the limpid air above us, it seemed a benign augury, returning our salute with the chapel bell, tinkling in the silence.

The next moment the engines paused suddenly and, with our momentum lost, the land wind swept across the ship. It brought the smell of thyme growing on those barren hillsides, the smell of land. Syros was alive. It had been called forth from the world of ghosts and fantasies. It existed.

A moment later, the land itself abandoned its long resistance to our ship. The promontory fell away and we turned the corner, into an audience of chalk white houses gathered around the harbor.

But the whistle was still sounding in my ears. For my father it was a benign greeting, a welcome home. For me it was the shrill apprehension of arrival on an unknown shore. The Greek Revolution began in

1821. Mine began in 1954, and that ship's whistle was the tocsin, the signal for the conflict to begin, for images to clash together, between a Greece that had been and a Greece that was.

We were driven up to the villa in the hills. At every turn the driver blew his horn, hardly slackening his speed, so that all the way up the winding road another insistent trumpet continued the alarm. Beyond the final turning we could see a rim of mountains unfold against the sky, and my mother pointed to lights in the distance beyond a cavernous valley.

It was the villa, still there after fifteen years. My grandfather was gone, and now the villa's mistresses were three Kasiot women, my mother's great-aunts, sisters of mother's grandmother. It was as though the compounded catastrophes of war and exile had simply reversed the normal pattern of inheritance so that the house was acquired not by the younger generation but by the older.

"They can see us," my mother said, for she knew, ever since the ship's whistle had sounded and the driver had descended to the town, that the three old women would be standing at the gate.

And they were. Three black shadows stood against the ornate latticed door, with a retinue of servants around them. They wore black robes blowing in the wind, and loose black cowls shrouding their faces.

They were my first view of Kasos, those three women, though it would be another ten years before I actually arrived there. I had my first glimpse of Kasos that night in Syros, as a boy of seventeen, arriving on this implausible summer excursion to confront three hooded figures on a hilltop of the past.

In the weeks to come I understood that my aunts, too, were strangers in Syros. Their black robes and cowls set them apart from the rest of the population; they spoke Greek in an unfamiliar accent and used words the Syriots did not understand.

Even these three old women were living out a *xenitia*. They themselves were in exile, and the surrounding hills of Syros were as irrelevant to them and to their place of origin as the hills of Westchester had been to my parents. In my journey to the past, I had reached only a way station, the same one my grandparents had reached, arriving in Syros from the opposite direction.

So my arrival in Syros was a false arrival. Syros was a vantage point from which another journey extended outward, toward an island that could be imagined only beyond the remaining expanse of time and sea.

But that summer I got no farther. I returned to a final year in an American school, headed for an American college. There followed more years of *xenitia,* and the black Kasiot grandams receded again into the world of dream. I was twenty-seven when I set out again, resolved to make the journey to its end.

In the meantime I managed to learn more about Greece. Once I discovered it was actually a country, I began to read about it the same way I might read of France or England. I started with the present and read backward, a natural method as the first Greece I knew was downstairs in my house. In the same way, I learned more of the Greek language, giving form to countless sounds and syllables that had existed amorphously in my mind.

"Do you speak Romaic?" asked the familiar strangers in my father's house.

At first I didn't know what to answer. If they meant did I speak Greek, I would have made a brave attempt to get the endings right and said: "Yes, I speak Greek." But what was Romaic? I had never heard of it. I shook my head, and they laughed and said "Shame on you, not to speak Romaic."

Finally, they asked me so many times that I began to suspect *Romaic* must have something to do with *Greek*. When they asked me again, I said, "Yes, I speak Romaic." So they smiled and said, "*Bravo*, you're a good boy who speaks Romaic."

After that I troubled my head no more over the meaning of *Romaic*. It was just another word for Greek, which adults had used perversely to confuse me. Then I learned that Romaic is the language spoken by modern Greeks, as distinguished from the Hellenic of the ancients. After the fall of Constantinople, the citizens of the fallen Byzantine Empire were known to their Turkish masters as Romaioi (Romans) and their language as Romaic.

"*Ti haparia?*" I heard my parents say to friends in greeting. "What *haparia?*" or as I translated by intuition, "What news?" As good a mimic as any child, I echoed what I'd heard: "Hello," I said to parents' friends, "*Ti haparia?*"

Eventually, I learned the word *hapari* does mean news, but it is a Turkish word, which in its original meaning was applied strictly to news of death. So, taking the etymology far enough, what I was really saying in those cheerful greetings of my childhood was: "What news of death can I expect from you? Who do you know in Charon's kingdom now?"

In the same way I began to unravel stories I had been hearing all my life, stories of events that had taken place on Kasos in my grandparents' time and earlier.

Most of my father's brothers were born on Kasos, and with these relatives visiting my house in Rye, I had ample opportunity to hear of it. I learned much from my parents too, for in a Greek family stories have a way of being handed on. Though my parents had never lived in Kasos, they could tell me what they had learned of it from their own parents and grandparents.

In this way, I assembled what I know of Kasos, adding something here and there, until some pattern of the island must emerge, like the mosaics made of smooth black and white pebbles on the floors of the island courtyards.

At last, I made a journey to the island myself, an actual journey. To make it, I needed a guide and mentor, for on any journey of discovery, the traveler needs someone to accompany him who knows the way. For me, this guide and mentor was the eldest of my father's brothers, Uncle George. He had come to New York when we did. Before that, he had arrived in London at the same time as my father and grandfather. And before that, he had made the emigration to Syros.

For unlike my parents, he was born in Kasos at the end of the nineteenth century, and when his father and mother journeyed northward a few years later,

Uncle George was a boy of seven, watching Kasos disappear behind him.

It is hard to imagine him as he was then, so I must start with what I first remember of him in Rye, New York. As we played in our yard on a summer afternoon, my brothers and I would hear the sound of digging. Then, above the hedge that enclosed the vegetable garden, Uncle George would rear up from his labors. He wore overalls like the Farmer in the Dell; his shoulders were stooped and his cherub face was glowing with the heat and the merry embarrassment of being discovered at some mischief.

"Ah, there you are, Uncle George!" we said.

And Uncle George replied, "Yes, there you are Uncle George!"

To tease us, he used to call us all Uncle. "Uncle Stathe," he called my brother, which made Stathe very angry.

"I'm not *Uncle* Stathe," my brother would protest. "I'm just plain Stathe."

And Uncle George, too, was just plain Uncle George. We would see him tramping across our lawn on a Sunday morning in his baggy business suit, with the belt buckled up high around his waist, his shoulders rounded in a perfect curve.

"You'll stay for lunch, Uncle George," we said, taking him by the hand.

"No, I cannot," Uncle George would say, holding back, beaming with mischief.

"Why not, Uncle George?"

"Because you have no food."

"But we do! We do, Uncle George."

"You do?" said Uncle George. "Well, then I'll stay."

He lived in New York City, at the Delmonico Hotel on Park Avenue. Most often, he would come out to Rye by train, wearing his rumpled suit and carrying a large bundle of newspapers under his arm. And as soon as he arrived, he would leave the grown-ups upstairs and come down to the basement to enter the magic fraternity of our childhood. Sometimes he would bring some contraption with him, some quixotic project we would pursue with him for an entire Sunday afternoon. Once it was a parachute he had bought from Army-Navy surplus.

"You're not going to make the children jump off the roof, are you?" my mother said.

"Of course not!" said Uncle George.

"Of course not!" we said, echoing his indignation, though with Uncle George, we weren't entirely sure.

But Uncle George was true to his word. Instead, out of the attic window, fastened to the straps of the parachute, he threw out one of my father's best leather suitcases.

On another occasion, he brought a kit for making plaster statues: a quantity of rubber to be melted down and made into a mold, and a plaster composition to be made into the statue. Uncle George borrowed a saucepan from my mother, then led us to a workshop in the cellar. He stood over the pan of bubbling rubber like a sorcerer.

"I know," he said. "We'll make a copy of Stathe's cat."

Uncle George remembered seeing a porcelain cat in my brother's room, and he asked Stathe to bring it. As we two sorcerer's apprentices looked over his shoulder, Uncle George poured molten rubber over it.

The porcelain cat was ruined. Wherever it is today, it has a brown rubber stripe running down its back. But by the end of the afternoon, there were dozens of other cats to take its place, dozens of white plaster likenesses, all imperfect copies of the original.

With each new birth, Stathe or I would run upstairs to show it to our parents. One cat had no ears, another no tail. There were blind cats, lame cats, headless cats. They came out of our cellar like a plague.

Stathe hurried back to the workshop where the kindly wizard was continuing his work.

"No more cats," said Stathe.

"What?" said Uncle George.

"My mother says no more cats. She says we already have too many cats."

And so we did. There were cats on every table, by every chair. They lurked behind sofas, stood brazenly on doorsteps. As creator of that bizarre litter, Uncle George felt he must make amends.

"We'll take them to church," he said.

"What for?"

"So the ladies can sell them at the spring bazaar."

It was no use. When the bazaar was over, all the cats came back, each one swaddled in newspaper. The ladies of the parish thanked us but regretted to inform us that not one cat had been sold.

With such a record of quixotic adventure, Uncle George was bound to come on my journey. He had no responsibility for the project, as I was the one to initiate it. But he took a certain risk in helping me.

He told me so much about the Kasos of his parents' and grandparents' day that, like the cats he let out of our cellar, some things might return to haunt him.

In the summer of 1964, he set out with me for Kasos. By that time he was living in Greece, working in a shipping office in Piraeus. After twenty years in London and another twenty in New York, he had turned his outward journey back upon itself. Now, accompanying an insistent and inquiring nephew, he would retrace that journey to Kasos, its first point of departure.

To get to Kasos we had to take a ship from Crete. There were three of us, Uncle George and I and my cousin, another Elias, son of my father's brother John, who was born and raised in London. Like most Greek first cousins who are eldest sons, he and I have the same first name because we are both named for our father's father, Captain Elias, who lived in Kasos with his wife, Eleni.

When we arrived in Crete, we realized that we had no presents to bring our Kasiot hosts, some small token to commemorate our visit. Uncle George had a vast assortment of objects in his suitcase, for he was an incorrigible saver: plastic bags that had once enclosed new shirts, a bottle of cleaning fluid wrapped in a piece of heavy rubber tubing, an endless supply of cotton, pencils, toothpicks, and bits of rubber bands. But nothing suitable for presents.

As the journey neared its end, we were dreading what the Kasiots would have to say about us, the satirical couplets called *mandinadhas*, sung to the lyre in the café, which they would compose about our stinginess. Then we saw a clump of bananas hanging in front of a fruit vendor's shop.

We stopped the car and Uncle George got out.

"Shall we buy them?" he asked. When Uncle George asked such a question, the idea would chase itself around in his head for a while and nothing you could say would make any difference.

We bought the bananas. I was chosen to take charge of them, as I had just cleverly rearranged my luggage to have one free hand. Now, in that free hand, I carried a giant clump of bananas to the car, a huge stalk with dozens of unripe bananas growing out of it.

"Well, at least we'll have some presents now," I said to my uncle as the car started up again. "When we come ashore in Kasos, I can carry the banana tree and you can break off the bananas and pass them out among the people."

"You think so?" replied my uncle. "That would be worse than no presents, since obviously they would misunderstand and compose even nastier couplets at our expense."

Now Uncle George is never one to explain what he means. If you do not understand, he will just wait for you to ask him and then supply an explanation. But by that time, I had asked him so many questions that I was beginning to feel like Glaucon in the dialogues, posing ingenuous questions as cues for Socrates.

On the subject of bananas, it was time for such a cue.

"Why, Uncle?" I asked.

"Why?" said Uncle George. "I'll tell you why."

And so, Socratically, my uncle explained that in

the islands, as well as in the rural areas of mainland Greece, it was indecorous to mention anything of phallic shape. A peasant, speaking of a cucumber or a squash, would feel he owed his listener an apology.

"Begging your pardon," he would say, "the cucumbers in our village grow to be that long." Or, "Our squashes—by your indulgence—are not out yet."

Now things took a turn for the worse, as I saw the true significance of that phenomenon rearing up beside me on the seat. If you could not mention a single banana in polite company, what could you say about an entire banana tree? What would I say when I disembarked at Kasos, risen from the sea, with a hundred bananas held on high?

In Iraklion, in Crete, as we waited for the boat for Kasos, I was wandering around in a museum of medieval Greek history when I found a photograph of a ridge of mountains taken from a distance across a high plateau. Beneath it there was the caption: A view from Anoyia, looking toward the Kulukuna Range.

I led Uncle George to the photograph. He looked at it silently for several minutes.

"What are you suggesting?" he said.

For an answer, I put my finger over the final *a*, leaving the remainder, Kulukun.

"You may be right," said Uncle George.

Uncle Manuel, the middle brother, said our name meant The Man To Whom All Things Come, from the Arabic *kulu enta*. He said our ancestor, the first Elias of record, got a nickname during the Greek Revolution when he was taken prisoner as a slave sailor on board an Egyptian ship.

The officers used to amuse themselves by throwing coins in the air and making the Greek sailors jump for them. Old Elias caught so many coins that the Egyptians were always shouting, "Kulu enta! Kulu enta!" ("You got everything!") And they said it so many times that the nickname stuck.

Uncle George, on the other hand, maintained that the name came from *kuluki*, the Kasiot word for dog. It was obvious that my two uncles had different views of life and of themselves; and with his satirical irony, Uncle George delighted in commenting on Uncle Manuel's more exalted notions.

The origin of our name was one of the questions I wanted to answer on our trip to Kasos, but unexpectedly, I had found a clue here in Crete before we had even arrived at our final destination.

The possibility became compelling when I remembered that some Greek names are formed to mean the one who comes from a certain place. Halkitis is the man from Halki, Roditis the one from Rhodes. In every case, a *tis* is added to the place to make the person who comes from there. Kulukunatis would sound awkward to the native ear. Much simpler to drop the *a* and add the *tis* directly to the stem, arriving at Kulukuntis (Kulukundis, begging your pardon).

At last we found it. All things come to him who waits, and every dog will have his day. My uncles had been searching for a nickname, simply because they could not find the name in any of the other categories. They had not suspected that the name, though Greek, might not be a nickname but a place-name after all.

Old Elias, or some ancestor of his, must have been

a Cretan, a native of that region in the Kulukuna Mountains. Perhaps he journeyed eastward to Kasos and, remembering the valley of his childhood, he spoke of it so often that the people of his adopted country thought of him as the one who came from the Kulukunas.

During the Greek Revolution of 1821, he might have been among the twenty-five hundred Cretans who took refuge in Kasos. He might have been one of those crouching beside the native Kasiots at the rampart. Then, in the debacle that followed, he was taken prisoner by the Egyptians and put to work as a slave sailor on an Egyptian ship. And the rest of the story is remembered history.

In the time remaining before the boat, we set out for the Kulukunas, (Uncle George took the matter seriously) and on the way we could not resist performing some experiments. Stopping in villages along the road, we first asked how would the villagers call someone from the Kulukunas? And when that failed, did they know of anyone named Kulukundis?

But we were almost at the Kulukunas themselves before anyone had heard of them. The Kulukunas are a hump of land standing across a valley that opens from the northern slopes of Mount Ida. That was another disappointment. They were discouragingly small. They were not even mountains, but hills: brief interruptions in the level of the land. They hardly had time to rise to their pitiful height before they sloped again down to the sea.

Nearby was the village of Perama, on the main highway from Iraklion to Rethymnon, and then

Melidhoni, between Perama and the sea. We sat down in the café on the square in Melidhoni and the entire male population gathered around us.

"How do you people call yourselves?" I said, to start things off.

Thirty faces looked at me.

"How do you refer to yourselves when you speak to people from other places?"

More silence and blank looks.

"Melidhonites!" someone said at last, and instantly a murmur of relief passed around the assembly. Yes, they were Melidhonites.

"Just Melidhonites?" I said. "Don't you think of yourselves as people from this entire region? Aren't you also people from the Kulukunas?"

But having discovered their name, they were not to be deprived of it so easily.

"No," the spokesman said firmly. "All people from Melidhoni are Melidhonites and all people from the Perama are Peramites."

"That may be true," I said. "But I think all you Melidhonites and Peramites are also people from the Kulukunas and therefore you could all be Kulukundises!"

They looked at me as though I was insane.

"We have no such names here," someone said.

I turned on him instantly. "What do you mean? What names?"

"No names like that," he said. "Like Kuluk . . . or whatever you said. There is no single name for the entire region."

That was progress. He granted that Kulukundis could be a name that might be given to someone from

Kulukuna, if that had been the practice, despite the fact that, as he assured me, it wasn't the practice.

Going on to Perama, we asked so many questions of the café keeper that he sent for the schoolteacher, who was the town scholar. This man had been to study in Athens and could tell us everything. Soon the teacher appeared, blinking in the sudden sunlight. Obviously, he had been roused from his nap. We offered him a coffee and asked him what he knew.

But the schoolteacher had no clue how someone from the Kulukunas would be called. As a last resort, I posed the final question: Did he know anyone named Kulukundis?

His eyes brightened.

"Yes, I do," he said.

"Really?"

"Yes, yes," he said, enthusiastic now that he was finally able to help.

"Where does he live?" I said. I was enthusiastic too.

"There is not just one, there are many of them," he said.

"Where do they live?"

"They don't live here anymore. They have gone away."

"Gone away from the Kulukunas?"

"What *Kulukunas?* Gone away from Greece. They are a shipping family of five brothers, and they have all gone away to England and America."

So my theory remains a conjecture.

When at last we arrived in Ayios Nikolaos to take the boat for Kasos, Uncle George and I tried to do something about our bananas. We got a paper carton from the café owner and borrowed a jackknife from an American tourist. Ruthlessly, Uncle George cut off all the bananas and packed them in the carton. Now I would not need to apologize as I stepped ashore at Kasos.

The tourist was amazed at us. Why were we cutting off the bananas? It's a long story, I thought. Where did those bananas come from? He had never seen such tiny ones. Doesn't matter, I thought, size has nothing to do with it.

The ship set out at dawn. Beyond the eastern tip of Crete, we crossed the straits the sailing ships had passed through with cargoes bound for Egypt. That was the unprotected stretch of sea where during the Revolution every captain unfriendly to the cause of Greece cast an uneasy eye around him, dreading to see a speck on the horizon turn into a Kasiot ship, approaching to attack.

But now the sea was empty. Crete was fading behind us, and ahead there was horizon all around, vacant and unbroken. I was on the bridge with Uncle George, waiting for Kasos to materialize.

In a low murmur, every so often obliterated by the wind, he explained the principles of navigation. He must have been remembering other days at sea, imagining that after the outward voyage of his life, he was navigating this homeward landfall himself.

But my mind was not on navigation. It was on the horizon ahead of us. I knew we must be halfway, and because the coast of Crete had disappeared behind us, Kasos should appear at any moment.

For an instant I thought I saw a rim of mountains

outlined against the sky, a penciled curve against the obscure confluence of sky and sea. But when I blinked, the line was gone. I saw nothing but the light mist that hung on the horizon like the vapors of the morning. Even now, if it was there at all, Kasos was a phantom.

Suddenly, it was there. It had become, out of that obscurity of sky and sea, exactly the form of that first elusive vision. It grew more distinct, emerging from the heat blur on the horizon. As we came closer, we saw waves breaking on the rocky coast, marking the boundaries of the land with an unbroken ring of white, showing the sense of the ancient name the Phoenicians had given it: Kas, the isle of sea-foam.

We saw coves and turnings on the impenetrable coast, the land cascading sharply into bottomless blue water. The island itself appeared completely bald, like a mountain peak, which in fact it is. Halfway up the northern coast, we saw the first signs of life: dry-stone walls protecting each narrow strip of land from ravages of the goat; and abandoned mills, shorn of blades, marching up the barren slopes in a decapitated phalanx. At last we saw houses, tiny white squares dotting the top of a hill like gravestones.

We approached the landfall obliquely, making for a set of islands off the northern coast. As we neared them, they separated one behind the other, like unjoining bones. Past Armathia, the largest island, we turned to starboard, aiming for a small harbor, still invisible, the Bucca, which I knew to be the only niche in the ironbound Kasiot coast.

Along the shore was a group of houses, which I knew must be the town of Phry. Beyond, we could see the other towns: Panayia, Poli, Arvanitohori, and Ayia Marina, all laid out on that scant plateau beneath the mountains like eggs in the corners of an apron.

Remembering the landfall at Syros, I waited for the town of Phry to unfold around the harbor. As we came closer, I thought the houses were a suggestion of the town, the rear turned seaward. They were all low and square, some a faded white, others grayish brown. Some were the ghosts of houses: empty windows in a four-walled frame, enclosing nothing but the rubble of a caved-in roof.

These were the husks of houses, the life shelled out of them, not by war or earthquake, but, surely and inevitably as either one, by time and *xenitia*. At the center were two breakwaters, with a narrow passage between them leading into what had served for centuries as the only harbor on the island: the Bucca, named after the Italian word for mouth, sealed off from the sea by threatening jaws.

Beside the Bucca, on a rocky and embattled bastion, the Church of St. Spiridon presided with a bell tower of faded red, yellow, and blue, with a clock on its face marking the morning hour as incongruously as though it had been stopped for a hundred years.

We proceeded to the landfall, engines throbbing in the sudden silence, the sea audibly washing the iron coast a hundred yards or so away. We aimed a little east of the church and houses, where the entrance to the harbor must be. I thought we would round a promontory and make the turn as we had at Syros, and there would be an audience of houses suddenly revealed.

But the turning never came. There was no promontory for us to sail around, and there was no more to Phry. The houses trailed off into a stony wasteland. A dirt road, almost indistinguishable from the earth, wound on farther toward an unattended harbor.

The only audience for this landfall was a disorderly procession of people taking long silent strides toward the harbor, shielding off the sun with parasols and kicking up the dust. Five hundred yards later, without a turning, the ship slipped into the narrow receptacle that was our journey's end. At that moment, two jet planes of the Greek Air Force flew over the island before turning north to Rhodes: two scraping anachronisms, disfiguring an imagined sky.

We made our way through the chaos on the wharf. Under one arm, I carried a reel-to-reel tape recorder, what was called portable in those days. Under the other, balancing precariously, I held a boxed and corded cargo of forbidden fruit.

To get to my grandmother's house, we took one of the two taxis on the island. Another clarion sounded through narrow streets. Chickens, goats, and donkeys fled before us. Children ran to stand beside their mothers, watching from doorways. As the town thinned out, the crumbling foundations sank once again into fields of rubble.

The car rattled uphill, then stopped before a row of dilapidated balconies overlooking the sea. At the end of the row, by a light blue doorway in a wall of gypsum white, I saw my grandmother's house.

It was the house where Uncle George and three of his brothers were born. No one in the family had lived there since my grandparents Captain Elias and Eleni and four small boys embarked on that first emigration north to Syros.

It was really two houses, with a veranda between them, presiding over a courtyard below. Around the whole compound there was a high wall with a wooden gate leading to the street. The walls were all of blinding white gypsum, baked by the sun of a hundred summers. The wooden doors and shutters were painted light blue, so that the whole house was a sort of Greek flag—light blue and white—a motif that must have rankled Kasos's erstwhile rulers, the Turks and the Italians.

At the gate an old woman greeted us. She used to be Uncle George's nurse, brought originally from an orphanage to look after Eleni's first four children. She had left the family just after the emigration to Syros, to live out her own *xenitia* in Alexandria.

Fifty years later, impoverished and arthritic, she returned to her adopted home in Kasos and lived alone in the house of the blue shutters. She called it "my Eleni's house" though Eleni had long departed this life and she, the old woman, was its only mistress.

For our arrival, she wore a bright, checkered robe, a white kerchief around her head, and thick, gogglelike lenses. Her name—no more appropriate to the plump and saucy island girl than to the wrinkled woman on bandaged and arthritic feet—was Aphrodite.

"So you've decided to come," Aphrodite told my uncle. "And who are these you've brought?"

"Two Eliases," said Uncle George. "Sons of my brothers. Elias of John. And Elias of Michael."

Our lineage made no impression on her. She hadn't known our fathers, for they were the last of Eleni's sons, born in Syros after the emigration.

"So the two Eliases have come to Kasos too," she

said, and turned inside the gate. Two silent Eliases entered after her.

She led us through the courtyard, beneath the two white houses presiding over it, up the stone stairway to the terrace between them, with smooth black and white Rhodian pebbles, set by a traveling mosaic maker in the shape of a flower. From this terrace, which is like the bridge of a sailing ship, you could sweep your eyes across the Aegean Sea.

Aphrodite dismissed it with a wave of her hand. "You should have come to Alexandria," she said. "There I had a house of my own to live in, and another one that I made into a boardinghouse with Arab servants to wait on me and call me Kyra Aphrodite. And then, my bad luck, I got sick so I couldn't run the house anymore, and I didn't have any money, so I asked your uncle what I should do and he said, 'Go back to Kasos, go back to the old house.'"

"I said that?" said Uncle George. "On the contrary, I knew you'd be unhappy here but you insisted on coming back."

"I insisted on coming back? Why should I come back to this pile of rubble?"

It was an old dispute between them. I realized the relations one forms in childhood can endure a lifetime, and so for Uncle George, Aphrodite was not an old woman to be indulged and pitied, but rather the sharp-tongued island girl who had once led him to the washbasin by the ear. That explained why they quarreled about everything.

We went into the second house, where no one—not even Aphrodite—had lived since 1899. We followed its custodian, as though entering a newly opened tomb. This house was built originally for Eleni's mother and was passed down to Eleni when she married.

It was built in the European style, without the raised sleeping platform and the latticed railing of the Turkish bedrooms. It had a living room called a *salla,* chairs and sofas instead of Turkish cushions, and designs on the walls and ceiling, painted by a traveling artist from Smyrna.

On one wall, framed and pressed under glass, was a piece of needlework, a skill every Kasiot maiden must master. Beneath it was Eleni's mother's embroidered signature and a date: Marigo Malliarakis, 1863.

Now, in the privacy of our house, with the doors closed and windows shuttered, we unpacked the bananas and spread them on the windowsill. In the days to come, some of them came to a mysterious end.

The next evening Aphrodite came in on her bandaged feet to explain that four bananas had slipped off the windowsill. They fell to the floor and rotted instantly, she said, so she had to dispose of them.

"Fine, Aphrodite, fine," said Uncle George, not paying much attention, but I wondered why she should make such a laborious and implausible explanation. The next afternoon, instead of going into the bedroom where I usually slept, I lay down on a sofa behind the doorway to the living room. My book had just slipped from my fingers. I was sinking into the moist and sultry somnolence of the Greek afternoon when suddenly I heard a padded step on the threshold.

It was Aphrodite, coming out of her room when she thought everyone was asleep, stepping lightly into the living room and the alcove where the bananas lay on the windowsill. I was motionless, watching her. She ate six bananas, peeled them one by one and devoured them almost whole. Then, licking her lips, she crept out again, like a sated wolf.

I was just thinking of what I would tell my uncle when there was another sound on the threshold and I closed my eyes again. It was another visitor braving that pitiless hour of the afternoon. This one was in his undershirt. His belt was buckled high above his waist, and his back was rounded in a perfect curve as he filled already puffy and cherubic cheeks with that unmentionable yet celebrated fruit.

On our first afternoon in Eleni's house, we found photographs in an old safe manufactured in Marseilles, and letters stuffed among silverware and crockery packed in wedding chests. But the greatest treasure we discovered was a photograph known in my family as the *Hectodactylon:* literally, the Sixth Dactyl.

It was of my uncle, taken according to the Kasiot custom of photographing a newborn baby so that the gender is apparent. My uncle had bare feet, his skirt was raised slightly, and his foot was drawn up between his legs—so that a careful scrutiny revealed a sixth toe.

When we went out onto the terrace above the courtyard, the sky was reddening toward Crete. Across from us, the mountains of Karpathos rose from the sea in a nimbus of mist.

"Look down there," said Aphrodite, pointing to the courtyard. The stones were cracked, and a huge stump protruded among them, marking the place where, in my uncle's childhood, a large pine tree stood high over the house.

"Eleni was crowned in marriage here," said Aphrodite. "In this courtyard, Elias Kulukundis paid his call to the family of his future bride, concluding his engagement. A week later, they were crowned together beneath this sky, and this courtyard was all rice and sugared almonds.

"Then the first child was born, and the towns-people waited for the midwife to come out and stand on the terrace, holding the child against the sky. And according to the custom, she gave out a false announcement to deceive any evil spirits.

" 'It's a girl!' she said, though with the child held naked above them, everyone could see it wasn't so, that Eleni's firstborn was a man-child and his name was George!"

"Yes," I said to my cousin, the other Elias, "with a sixth toe to prove it."

"Later," she continued, "the christening was held within these same four walls. The priest came up from St. Spiridon to perform the service. And someone on the balcony—I forget who—picked up a handful of *mezitia* (Turkish coins) and flung them into the sky above the courtyard, so that on George's christening, the sky was raining money.

"And let me tell you, that was the last time it has been raining money anywhere near your uncle. He's so stingy, he can't find a pound or two to keep the walls and shutters painted on his mother's house."

"Stingy?" came Uncle George's voice from the living room. "I'm always sending you money, more than you know what to do with."

The wind came up, and across from us the peaks of Karpathos had vanished into the mist. We went inside to sit in the *salla* of Marigo Malliarakis, where a reactivated chandelier glowed with a somber, unsteady light.

Uncle George sat at the table, musing over photographs. My cousin and I sat beside him. Around us, Aphrodite hovered on silent feet. She would not sit but pretended to have some imaginary errand. Now she was moving piles of letters from one table to another and back again.

"Come back to Kasos, have you?" she said. "You've taken your own advice and come here with your two nephews. But what you expect to find here, I do not know. Whatever it is, you won't find it, and next week, when the ship comes from Crete again on her way to Rhodes, you'll sail away. What do you want with a poor forsaken island, you and your nephews from England and America?

"But you take an old woman who had a life of her own in Alexandria, who had a boardinghouse where only English people stayed, and Arab servants who talked to her in Romaic and called her Madame Aphrodite, and you tell her 'Go to Kasos. Stay in the old house. It is better for you.' "

"I never told you to go back. You wanted to."

"Yes, I wanted to come back. Because I thought it was Kasos I would be coming back to. I thought I would be coming to the island I had left. How did I know there was no Kasos anymore?

"Better for me, you say? Yes, thank you very much. Better for me to shut myself up in my tomb so I won't have far to go when death comes. Better for me to lie down here and wait for them to come and take me on the sheet. Better for me? Maybe I'll go and throw myself in the sea. That would be better for me too."

"Oh, stop," my uncle said. "Is that your way to welcome us?"

"Oh, I forgot. Welcome to you. Welcome to Kasos. Welcome to a Kasos that isn't here. This is not Kasos, so why should I welcome you? Kasos was here when the sky was all red in the west and it wasn't sunset. Kasos was here when the sky was all glowing over Crete and the hour was midnight. That was Kasos, when we all woke up because there was wailing and moaning in the town as though for death, and we went down to the Bucca and saw the sky all on fire over Crete with the flames of revolution.

"That was Kasos, when a boatload of Cretans sailed into the Bucca, and the five Turks who were living on the island went down to stop them, and they got as far as St. Spiridon and saw the Cretans with their swords and guns and they ran away and let them sail away again for Karpathos. That was Kasos.

"Kasos was when the *kaimakami* (the Turkish governor of the island) was living in the last house of Phry, where the road winds uphill to Ayia Marina, and he used to pass by this house on his way to meet the elders of the island, and he would walk under that balcony of our house, painted all light blue to go with our white walls for very spite of him, and he would call up, in Romaic, 'Good morning, Kyra Eleni.' And my Eleni would call down to him, in Romaic (just as I'm talking to you), 'Good morning, Mr. *Kaimakami.*' "

At that moment, looking under the table, Aphrodite caught sight of my tape recorder with its plastic reels gleaming as they turned.

"Christ and Virgin, will you look at that!" she said. "There is a genie listening to us! All the time we're talking, there's a demon underneath the table, listening to every word we say. Holy Virgin! As if we don't have enough trouble on this island, we have this nephew from America who brings a genie to catch our words! Now, will someone please tell me again: Whose child is that?"

"Michael's," said my uncle. "My brother Michael's."

My cousin laughed at that, and Aphrodite looked at him as though seeing him for the first time.

"What are you laughing at, my boy? Do you understand what we are saying? George, do these children understand Romaic?"

"Of course they do," my uncle said. "That one is writing a book, and he's brought his tape recorder to listen to every word you say. And when he returns to America, he's going to write it all down, so the whole world can hear your foolishness."

"Kyrie Eleison!" said Aphrodite, making the sign of the cross. "Then I won't say anything. I'll be silent as the grave."

She was silent for one moment.

"Come back to Kasos, have you? Come back with your nephew and his demon. But there is no Kasos here. There is only this abandoned rock with its roofs fallen in and its houses empty. There are no people living here, only goats and donkeys. It's an island of asses you returned to. Not to Kasos, not the Kasos I have known. And you, my nephew from America, let me tell you."

She turned to me now, her thick lenses flashing the light of the chandelier into my eyes.

"Son of Michael, if you had been in Kasos when your grandparents were newly married, then you would have seen it. Let me tell you about that Kasos."

So the muse sang to me of Kasos, of a Kasos that had been and was no more. She sang of fifty sailing ships anchored in the lee of Makra Island, of caïques plying the windy passage with seamen coming home. She sang of the grape harvest, and of planting time in November, when the Karpathian women, in their white robes and cowls, came to Kasos to work in the fields.

She sang of the feast days of the island saints, of violins, *laouts* and lyres, of the *sousta* danced by young men and women in a line. She sang of Palm Sunday, when everyone went to church to get a cross of palms, which was good protection from the "Evil Eye."

She sang of Good Friday when the bell tolled at sundown and the elders carried the tomb of Christ through the streets, and twelve priests followed in their black robes of mourning, chanting solemnly. Of the island lamentress, who wailed the dirges for the dead and that night would wail the saddest dirge of all, in a voice as piercing as a violin: "Where is there a ravine to hurl myself, where is there a sea to drown me? Where is there a razor to cut down my hair, a mother's hair whose Son is on the Cross?"

"My son of Michael," she said to me, "on Holy Saturday, you would have been on the square before the church with everyone on Kasos, the island all quiet, with only the waves pounding in the darkness. You would have seen the priests come out in golden robes instead of black, one of them carrying the lighted candle, passing the light to the congregation. You would have seen the light handed on from candle to candle until the whole square was bright.

"And beyond the Bucca, you would have seen all the ships of Kasos come from Makra Island to stand at anchor in a line, their masts and rigging aglow with torches. You would have seen the island illuminated and heard the joyful song of the Resurrection, 'Christ Is Risen from the Dead.'

"You would have heard that song and sung it yourself, along with your grandfather and grandmother and all the natives of your island. You would have seen all the people returning to their houses, candles flickering on all the roads and in all the windows of the island. 'Christ is risen from the dead.'

"And that was Kasos, my son of Michael. That was the Kasos you would have known, if you had not arrived too late."

Uncle George and Aphrodite. (Photo by Robert McCabe)

THE WAY TO PHRY

On our first morning in Kasos, my uncle must have been thinking of his brother Basil. Basil is the lost brother, the only one of my father's brothers I have never called Uncle, the only one my father never knew because Basil died in 1907 and my father was born in 1906.

"Basil used to be very nimble and quick," said Uncle George, sipping the tea Aphrodite had brought with our breakfast. "We used to take voyages on my father's sailing ship, the *Anastasia*. The first mate was my father's cousin Mavrandonis. We took his cabin so that he had to sleep in the chart room. Once Mavrandonis was about to put on a new bowler hat, but Basil ran in suddenly, took the hat, and floated it in a trough of soapy water where Aphrodite used to wash the clothes.

"Afterward, Basil became very quiet. Perhaps that was the beginning of his illness. He began to shake, his sight gradually diminished, and his head declined to the right. Father came home to Syros with his ship the *Anastasia*. He had been in the Black Sea where there was cholera, and he was placed under quarantine and couldn't come ashore.

"Mother went to the Port Office to confer with him. Should she take Basil to Athens for an operation? Apparently, by that time, they knew it was a tumor of the brain. But what could father say? What did he know? He said, 'Do whatever God reveals to you.'

"My mother decided to have the operation, and she took Basil to Athens. We did not go with him, first because of the expenses of such a journey, and then because we had school. Basil was in good spirits as he left. He wore a peaked cap, which Father had brought. Actually, Father had meant it for me, but I didn't like it, so to please Father, Basil wore it himself. And he wore it that day, on the long journey."

Uncle George said no more. After breakfast we put on bathing suits under our clothes and prepared to walk the two miles from our house to Ammoua, the only sandy beach on Kasos. We set out along a footpath, high above the sea, leading westward from the town of Phry on the northern shore.

The last Phrydiot houses thinned away. Below we could see a pool of salt water, called "the lake," a few yards from the sea, fed by waves breaking on the iron coast. We walked on, leaving the town behind us, past plots of earth enclosed in their walls of stone: grim fortresses against the indomitable goat, a vine or two growing in their citadel. We walked past a derelict mill, high above the sea: a stone turret, crippled and blind, its blades looted and sold for firewood.

Uncle George thought of Yeroyiannis and his *tsifliki,* or large estate, which he had seen somewhere along this path in his childhood. He walked ahead, his trousers belted high, a bath towel wrapped around his head for shelter from the sun. Suddenly he stopped and looked back at me with his black sunglasses wrapped in a shroud of white cloth.

"And so old Yeroyiannis's son
Made himself two *tsiflikia*.
The one is full of *lapatha*,
The other full of *fikia*."

Lapatha is a weed that grows inland; *fikia* grow near the sea. Like all estates in Kasos, whether inland or near the sea, Yeroyiannis's *tsifliki* was a kingdom of weeds.

We walked on past the small chapel of St. George of the Spring, in the craggy ravine of a rain torrent. The eulogy to Yeroyiannis's kingdom made slow repetitions as we walked. At Ammoua we had a swim. At the top of the hill above, we could see the houses of Ayia Marina, white and silent.

When we'd had our swim, we turned back on the way to Phry. The weather had cleared and Karpathos bloomed out of its membrane of white mist, so close that Kasos and Karpathos seemed one island, the sea like quicksilver poured into all its coves and turnings. Suddenly we saw a steamer turning silently in the empty sea: the *Arcadia,* the ship that brought us the day before, stopping in Kasos once again on its return journey from Rhodes to Crete.

It materialized like an apparition. And it made my uncle think of the day in 1898 when he and his younger brother Basil were walking on that very path, when the *Dhekeli,* the Turkish steamer from Alexandria, appeared on that empty disk with its *hapari*.

Uncle George was six years old and Basil was four. The year before there had been a disastrous war with Turkey, the year Aphrodite remembered when the

Cretan revolution reddened the horizon with fire and blood. When war broke out, the Dardanelles were closed to all Greek ships, and the *Anastasia,* bound for Russia with an unprofitable cargo of roof tiles, had to lay up in Syros. The family spent the winter with her: Captain Elias and Eleni, George and Basil, baby Nicholas, and Manuel in his mother's womb.

In the spring, when the war was over and the knot of Greek ships was loosened again in the Syros harbor, Captain Elias set out at last for the Black Sea to deliver the wretched roof tiles. After he picked up a cargo of grain for Alexandria, Eleni would accompany him on that journey because her brother, who was a doctor in Alexandria, had just become engaged and she wanted to be present at the *emvasmata,* the feast celebrating the engagement. That way, also, Eleni could see her sister Virginia, who had moved from Kasos to Alexandria.

On the way, they stopped at Kasos, to leave the older boys, George and Basil, in the care of Aphrodite and their grandmother Marigo.

They stayed long enough to take the two boys ashore, the *Anastasia* anchoring in the lee of Makra Island because the north wind was blowing and the ship could not anchor near the unprotected Kasiot coast. The caïque must have gone out to meet her, across the windy passage, plying the waves as stubbornly as a donkey.

And the whole town of Phry must have been watching as the caïque returned with Eleni and her two sons, the boys' shaven heads poking up from the stem like balls: two frightened, diminutive cavaliers riding the white horses home to Phry.

They were left to the tender mercies of their grandmother, Eleni's mother, who lived to have great-grandchildren yet hated children. Marigo was illiterate, and the letters of her name on the needlework tapestry must have been drawn for her by someone else, and she must have stitched them with no more comprehension than she would have had of the curls and spirals of Arabic.

But her husband, Vasilios Mavroleon, was highly educated. He was a merchant, a shareholder in sailing ships, though he himself was not a captain; and he was elected *demogeront* (distinguished elder) from the town of Phry. Vasilios thoroughly documented the transactions of his life, and there is no telling what resources he might have left us family historians if his archives had not met calamity.

Marigo, Old Yia-Yia, as we family historians called her, had an abhorrence of old papers, which my uncle swears has been passed down to all the females of the family, including, mysteriously, those who married into it. After her husband's death, year by year, for the remainder of her life in the house with the blue shutters, she tore out pages of the old man's ledgers, fastened them in a little loose-leaf binder, and hung them on a nail in the outhouse across the courtyard. My uncle, visiting that chamber when he came back to Kasos in 1910, found installments of the old man's records doomed to a service Vasilios had not foreseen.

To this gentle humanist the boys were consigned. She would put them to bed while the sun was still high in the sky, lock the door of the bedroom, and go visiting. On these nights, George was frightened. It was cold in the bed alone with Basil, for they were used to their mother sleeping with them. And then, before the advent of electricity, the streets were full of horrible imaginings: *striglas* and Nereids, and women who had died in childbirth and were thought to rise.

Sometimes a dog, glutted and crazed with eating lambs, would howl weirdly. And once, the mad girl of Phry, who went around wearing a coarse blanket and her father's underclothes, came up the stairway from the street, calling their mother, who was not there but in Alexandria, "Kyria Eleni! Kyria Eleni!"

Their parents had gone to Alexandria, to be present at the *emvasmata* of Eleni's brother, the Uncle-Doctor, as the boys called him. My uncle remembered him distinctly from a picture he saw only once: the Uncle-Doctor with his handlebar mustache sitting with his fiancée in the first row of a family portrait, taken by a professional photographer of Alexandria—not at an engagement or at a wedding but, unexpectedly, around Virginia's open coffin.

Years later, in Syros, my uncle pieced it together. He was with a friend from school, doing an experiment with sulfuric acid, and in his mother's hearing he pronounced the word *aqua-fortis*. When his mother heard that, she drew in her breath sharply and made a hissing sound, which meant that George had just said something very bad. "God forgive her," she muttered. And George knew by that evidence that what Aphrodite had told him was true: Aunt Virginia, his mother's sister, had poisoned herself in Alexandria with *aqua-fortis*.

My uncle saw Aunt Virginia only once. He was sitting on the courtyard wall of the house in Kasos while Aunt Virginia was coming across the courtyard, dressed in a pink robe, with her hair beautifully done. Then the mischievous, shaven imp—my uncle—greeted her with an obscene remark, which she ignored, as she stroked his hair.

That is all he remembered, except her umbrella with the thick handle of sculptured roses and the ivory fan, and the photograph taken by an open coffin.

One day, while Eleni and the Captain were still away, another aunt, Captain Elias's sister, took the boys to spend the day at her house in another part of Phry. Basil was so unhappy in the new surroundings that he cried all the time and would not eat. He wanted Aphrodite, so the aunt let them go home after lunch, and George took his younger brother by the hand and led him back through the devious streets of Phry. They had no trouble finding the house because of the Norfolk Island Pine tree in the courtyard. There were only two in all Kasos—one at their aunt's house and one at their mother's—and the two of them stood high above the town of Phry like two masts above a ship.

When they arrived, they found the door locked. No one answered though George too, joining Basil, was calling, "Aphrodite, Aphrodite!" The family was at Vasilios's summerhouse on the outskirts of Ayia Marina. Grandmother had gone there for the afternoon with Aphrodite, thinking the children were safe at their aunt's. At that hour of the afternoon, all the neighbors were asleep as the two children stood beneath the shuttered windows calling into the silent house, "Aphrodite, Aphrodite!"

George guessed where they must be, and he

thought he knew the way. He picked his way along
the stony path, Basil following, ominously silent now
when he should have been more anxious than ever for
his Aphrodite.

But George forgot to turn back down toward the
Bucca before turning up to Ayia Marina. Instead he
went down toward the sea, past the Chapel of St.
Nicholas, past the last Phrydiot houses where the path
winds out above the sea and you can see "the lake"
glistening below like a turquoise in a casing of stone.
Then, after the last Phrydiot houses thinned away,
they came to a solitary mill, blades hovering like a
becalmed sailing ship, and George remembered the
mandinadha Aphrodite had taught him about this
mill, which belonged to a man named Yeroyiannis:

"And so old Yeroyiannis's son
Made himself two *tsiflikia*.
The one is full of *lapatha,*
The other full of *fikia.*"

And now George knew there must be something
wrong, for this couldn't be the way to the summerhouse. The house was inland, but the path was winding downhill toward the shore. This was the way to
"the lake" for swimming, to St. George of the Spring,
the way to Ammoua. It was too late to change course.
George looked up and saw the town of Ayia Marina,
crowning the top of the hill; but to get there they
would have to climb through many fields, over many
crisscrossing dry-stone walls, into the blinding white
wall of the sun itself.

So they turned back on the way to Phry. Basil followed quietly, watching the steps and ledges in the
stone where he put his feet. The air had cleared and

Karpathos had bloomed suddenly out of the mist. It seemed so close that Kasos and Karpathos seemed one island, the sea surrounding it like quicksilver. Suddenly they saw the *Dhekeli,* the Turkish steamer, advancing silently, calling at Kasos weekly on its way through the Archipelago from Alexandria to Smyrna.

"Look George," Basil cried, "there's a *digla.*" He meant *strigla,* but he was only four. And George, too, found something magical about this ship. Its painted funnels seemed red hot, as though glowing with the fire of its engines. At the sight of it, they forgot the summerhouse. They quickened their steps, picking their way on the precarious path, racing to reach the Bucca in time to be there standing on tiptoe among the crowd on the breakwater.

But they had only reached Yeroyiannis's windmill when the whistle sounded. By the time they reached the town, the last caïques had been stuffed into the Bucca and Kasos was already gobbling all the news, relishing this weekly ingestion from the world beyond. There was the usual kissing and weeping, showers of black robes and cowls, litanies of welcome.

As George and Basil played among the luggage set out in the square in front of the Church of St. Spiridon, the sky was deepening. The smell of frying fish coming from the unshuttered windows made them know it was time to eat. And they made for home, through the devious Phrydiot streets, aiming for one of the two pines that rose above the town like masts. As usual, there were dogs barking, the whine of a lyre, the staccato of a grandmother calling a child. In addition, among all the other sounds, there was a slow, insistent wailing.

It became louder as they picked their way toward the pine tree. There was no one wailing in any house they passed. Instead there were silent faces at the windows: women and children. Now the wailing was louder still. As they started down the last row of Phrydiot houses lined up before the sea, the neighbors were on their balconies, watching them.

The front gate of their house was open and swinging, as were the door to the kitchen, the door on the balcony above, and all the shutters. George quickened his steps, leading Basil by the hand, for now he knew the wailing was coming from his house. The last time George had seen all the doors and shutters open was at the christening of his brother Nicholas or on his father's name day.

But this was not a christening and not a feast. The doors and windows of that house now hung loosely open, like a new widow who has cut the tight knot at the back of her head and for the first time let her hair hang down in mourning.

Aphrodite was at the gate. George had thought they could slip in unnoticed, up the stairs to the bedroom. But Aphrodite saw them before they could escape, and George put his head down like a donkey about to be beaten, Basil following. They stumbled through the doorway, their eyes shut and faces already wincing. But strangely Aphrodite did not seem to notice them.

"Charon, what did I do to you," a woman cried on the upper veranda, "that you took my little bird from me?"

"And dressed me," cried another, "in eternal black."

Behind them, he heard Aphrodite say, very politely, "Please come in. They are all upstairs."

And now George knew there were more visitors coming in behind them, and there was no turning back. Timidly, he led Basil toward the veranda. He hesitated at the corner of the house, because he always felt a moment of uncertainty when there were guests, even on a normal day.

He was always afraid the women would shriek and cackle and kiss him. For a moment, that was what he thought was happening, as he and Basil went around the corner. He thought it was for him, that sudden explosion of women's screams.

But no one looked at the boys as they took their places in that strange assembly. The women were sitting on cushions in a wide semicircle on the veranda floor. They were all in black, their cowls thrown back, their hair loose and hanging over their foreheads in two separate strands. The women were rocking and twisting as though there was something terrible hurting them.

They screamed and wailed and pulled ferociously on their locks of hair. Some of them were tearing at their dresses. Their black sleeves were shredded and they drew their nails mercilessly through the cloth and into their uncovered flesh.

Suddenly, the woman sitting closest to George and Basil stopped her wailing and turned to them with an eye as clear and cold as glass and said, "Sit down, children. What are you standing up for?"

George sat down at once, pulling Basil down with him on the same cushion. Now he looked more closely at the faces beneath those angry lashing curls, and he realized that every woman on the veranda was someone he knew. They were women of the neighborhood, women he had seen every day of his life. With their hair undone, they had seemed to be strangers.

At last, George felt his own inhaling breath make the sharp hissing sound as he realized that sitting in the semicircle was his grandmother Old Yia-Yia. Her cowl was thrown back and her hair hung over in two strands. Her black dress was torn and she was digging her nails into her flesh. George felt his breath taken away suddenly, and he had no breath to speak to her.

A single woman's voice rose up above the rest, as high as a violin. It was Kania, the midwife and exorcist, and also a lamentress for the dead, who sang the dirge of Christ every Good Friday, as the bier of Christ was carried through the smoky streets.

"Oh, miserable mother, you should have kissed your daughter's wedding crown," she cried. She was sitting in the center of the group, her face lifted to the sky. Around her the women sobbed in unison. They pulled at their separated braids of hair and gave short, stabbing cries of pain.

"Oh, miserable mother, you should have kissed your daughter's crown."

"Goo! Goo! Goo!" the women moaned in unison, pulling harder at their hair.

"Oh, miserable mother, you should have kissed your daughter's crown," she cried again, for the last time, the chorus responding, pulling harder, crying in rhythmic pain.

"And instead you kissed her forehead in the coffin."

Now the screams were not in unison. Each woman cried randomly as she tore at her hair and clothes and flesh. The bodies writhed and shuddered. Some of the women had torn open their dresses in front, uncovering their breasts, pulling and pinching.

The women all called different names. They were not wailing only for this mother, but each one was wailing for some kinsman she herself had kissed in death.

"Oh, my Yani, the bitter sea was your Communion!"

"Oh, my Nicola, black blood is flowing from my heart for you!"

Eventually, the waves of passion quieted. The women's heads fell forward on their breasts, their hands hung harmlessly at their sides. Their eyes were closed; their bodies swayed gently, throbbing into stillness. The entire circle was silent, heads bowed, like birds asleep.

Uncle George did not remember it, but according to Aphrodite, when Grandmother saw him and Basil, she got all excited and came after them as though to throw them down the cistern. Of course, it was just for show. Her idea was to take revenge on their mother, who had let Virginia die in Alexandria. Anyway, Aphrodite said, just to be sure, she locked them up in the bedroom until the wailing marathon was over.

And that was the last they ever heard of Aunt Virginia. Her story was buried with her body, to flower darkly once in Aphrodite's clandestine narration and once again, years later, in a sigh emanating from Eleni's soul. The only relics of her life were the ivory fan and the umbrella with its handle of sculptured roses, which Eleni kept with her always beside the icons of the house, and the photograph: an assembly of mourners gathered at an open bier.

I was shocked to see it, no less than I would have been to see the corpse itself, peeping up at us under the rising lid of an old wedding chest. It was the first such photograph I had ever seen, though they were as common as their opposites, the pictures of infants lately born.

That afternoon, after we returned from Ammoua, my cousin had seen an end of Aunt Virginia sticking out among dusty glassware and broken crockery in that place euphemistically called a living room. He got hold of her and pulled and kept pulling until out she came.

And then the whole house was in chaos—my uncle at the table, one astonished nephew over each shoulder, and Aunt Virginia supine on his knees. Around us, Aphrodite swooped and fluttered.

The picture showed an open coffin enclosing a young slender figure. The casket was tilted slightly, and the young woman's head was turned toward the camera. Her cheeks were round and youthful, the eyelids gently closed, her lips faintly touching in a suggestion of a smile. Around the forehead was a crown of lemon blossoms worn by a bride at her wedding. Behind her, along the length of the coffin, relatives stood in mourning: men in the stiff high collars of the time, women in black robes, bareheaded, their hair let down and parted in the middle in two separating locks.

"It's Virginia," my uncle said. "You see the crown?"

He explained for our sake. A married woman

might be buried with her wedding crown around her forehead. But an unmarried woman might also wear a crown to emphasize the poignancy of her untimely death, for of all bridegrooms, Charon was the one to win her.

"This is the picture I saw many years ago," my uncle said. "The one taken in Alexandria in 1898, which my mother kept all her life along with the ivory fan and the umbrella with the sculptured roses. And there, in the first row of mourners, you see my mother."

We looked again and, sitting directly behind the coffin, we saw Eleni. It was the only picture I had seen of her. She was dressed in black, bareheaded, her dark hair loosened and falling on either side of her face, not in angry lashing snakes, but in perfectly combed and orderly cascades of grief.

In her face there was no mark of violence or distorting passion. She was perfectly composed, glowing with the serenity of a woman complete in either joy or grief. She seemed unaware of anyone around her, her eyes resting on the cradled face before her in distant rapture.

But was my uncle right? Was it Virginia? Where was Uncle-Doctor and his fiancée? And where was Captain Elias, who should have been keeping vigil beside his wife? Perhaps these uncertainties began to trouble my uncle even then, though he said nothing, only gazed musingly at the photograph before him as one by one we left him to his own vigil by the corpse.

In the evening, my cousin and I were sitting on the terrace between the houses. There was silence all around us, except for the comforting background of an island's evening sounds. Before us, Karpathos faded in the darkness.

Suddenly, we heard noises that would not have been out of place on that terrace years before. We hurried into Uncle George's room, wondering what new *hapari* had arrived. There were no words, only noises, uttered with precision as though they were part of an intelligible language.

Uncle George was in his undershirt and slippers. Behind him, Aphrodite loomed. On his knees, he held another photograph, another corpse. A second one had surfaced on a new tide of old letters and broken crockery.

"Don't *you* have eyes to see, George?" Aphrodite asked. "I tell you it's a boy."

"How can it be a boy?" my uncle said, making a snap in his voice that should have meant the end of any argument.

"I'll tell you how," said Aphrodite. "Because it *is* a boy. Do you understand Romaic? Or shall I tell you in Arabic? It is a boy."

"How can it be a boy?" my uncle said. "Don't you see the wedding crown? You don't bury a boy with a crown around his head. I tell you it's Virginia."

We were crowding behind my uncle now. The photo was larger, of another casket, with no relatives behind it. Boy or girl, it was a young person: cheeks round and youthful, lips gently touching in another suggestion of a smile, around the forehead another crown of lemon.

"I don't know who it is," I said. "But there is one thing I *do* know."

To my surprise, they stopped shouting and looked at me.

"Whoever it is, it's the same person who's in the other picture, the one with the people all around it and Eleni sitting in the first row."

"And that's Virginia," my uncle said.

My cousin ran to bring the other picture. In a few moments, I knew the mystery would be undone. All the questions would be answered: the absence of Uncle-Doctor and his fiancée, the absence of Captain Elias.

We awaited my cousin now like Oedipus's second messenger, the one who offers no new knowledge, only a message that will join together two facts, bringing them to bear, inevitably and tragically, on a single person.

My uncle said nothing. He had taken off his glasses and was holding them like a magnifying glass against the sleeping face. Behind him, Aphrodite was quiet, waiting.

They were the same person. The same cheeks, robust in death, the same faint smile, the same crown of lemon. As we held the photos side by side, they fit one into the other, like the pieces of a puzzle.

Details emerged from the first photo we hadn't seen before, as though it had come suddenly into focus. How could we have missed them before? Didn't we have eyes to see?

Aphrodite was triumphant. "Look at the cap beside him," she cried, "and the brass buttons on his jacket. They buried him in his school uniform and his student's cap."

My uncle said nothing. His mind was whirling

The mysterious sleeper.

rapidly through the years and miles, misconception giving way to truth. It was not Alexandria in 1898; it was Athens in 1907. That was why Uncle-Doctor and his bride-to-be and Captain Elias were not there. That was why Eleni, curiously, was sitting beside the bier in the place reserved for the most bereaved of all, gazing at the face before her with the distant rapture of a Madonna Dolorosa.

My uncle knew, though Aphrodite could not have known, that it was not a student's cap the dead child had beside him. It was a peaked cap brought from Marseilles by Captain Elias for his first son George, the cap George had discarded and his younger brother, more dutiful than he, took up and wore. He had been wrong; it was a boy. It was his brother Basil.

It was the first time he had seen that photo, or any evidence of Basil's death. Basil had embarked on the final voyage, standing at the rail of the steamship, waving George's own cap at him in farewell. Life in Syros had closed over his departure like the sea. George was studying, looking forward to his exams when school would be over for the summer.

On the way back, the ship crept unseen around the promontory, with no sails of black to announce its deadly offering. George was coming home from school, wearing a blue flannel jacket with brass buttons, his books and papers under his arm. As he neared his house, he heard no wailing, saw no unshuttered windows and no flesh and clothing torn in grieving. Instead, he saw his brother John sitting on the wall. It was John who delivered the *hapari,* without emphasis.

"George," he said, with perhaps some challenge in his voice, some indecorous pride to be the one to bear his older brother such a piece of news, "Basil's dead."

We were all looking at the photograph. There was something uncanny about that sleeping face. The family resemblance was so great, it could have been Uncle George himself, in the uniform of the Syros high school, his own peaked cap laid beside him. As a musing man of seventy-two, Uncle George could have been gazing at his own thirteen-year-old corpse, mirrored back at him in some bizarre reflection.

"But the wedding crown," said Aphrodite, reminding us of the one detail yet unexplained. "Why did they bury him with a crown around his head?"

It was not a challenge. Her voice was reverent.

Unknowingly, she had brought to light the final evidence, the slender physical marking—the scars remaining on the ankles of the king—which alone will seal the tragedy beyond a doubt.

"Because of the wound," my uncle said, without passion. "Basil died in an operation for a tumor of the brain. In the open coffin, his wounded head would have been unsightly, so they bound it with a crown of lemon. He fought bravely and was crowned."

He fought bravely and was crowned.

Ὁ Λιμὴν τῆς Ἑρμουπόλεως ἐν ἔτει 1840 κατὰ χαλκογραφίαν παλαιοῦ περιηγητοῦ, ἀποκειμένην εἰς τὸ Δημαρχεῖον.

Syros in the nineteenth century.

A FEAST OF VENGEANCE

I hear you are writing a book about Kasos," said my father's first cousin, at a cocktail party in New York. "I hope you are going to include the story of my great-grandmother. She had an innocent man executed to avenge her husband's death, and when the executioner cut off his head, she raised the sword to her lips and drank her victim's blood."

She had not done that. The sword was passed to her before the execution, not afterward. The blood drinking is spurious, made up sometime in the century that followed the event, and it only shows how the woman's descendants held her in awe.

I heard her story in my childhood.

"She was a true virago," Uncle George said. "Pity and justice meant nothing to her, and she took her vengeance on an innocent man, concluding a vendetta."

Of that occasion in my childhood, I remember only those words heard for the first time: *virago, vendetta.* They had a ring of terror about them, but also a ring of exultation: a virago must be a wild, wicked woman, and Vendetta might have been the woman's name.

Years later, I asked Uncle George to tell me the story again. By that time I'd learned that vendetta was not a woman's name, but an honored ceremony based on the principle of a life for a life. In addition, the ancient Greeks believed that if a man was murdered and his death was not avenged, his body would not decompose in the grave but would rise to haunt the living. Although this belief originated with the ancients, since the Slavic migrations to Greece, the phenomenon has been known by a Slavic name, the *vrykolakas:* a creature rising from the grave to feed on the living, on the deceased's own family first of all.

In Greece the relationship between the living and the dead is a solemn one. The official period of mourning lasts for three years and in some rural areas the observance is so strict that during that time mourners may not be seen at any public celebration.

In those three years, the Orthodox religion prescribes memorial services to be held at certain intervals, for the soul of the deceased. Friends and family assemble in the church. The priests bless a honey cake and *kolyva,* a paste made of boiled wheat, honey, pomegranate seeds, nuts, and raisins. After the ceremony, these sweets are shared among the congregation in the dead person's memory so that in the conviviality of the occasion, any curses held against the dead man would be released.

The connection between the memorials and the fear of resuscitation becomes obvious when you consider that because of the scarcity of burial land in Greece, it was customary to exhume the body after three years and place the remains in an ossuary.

Thereafter, there would be no fear of resuscitation, and so the memorials were at an end.

The Virago was the mother of Old Yia-Yia, my great-great-grandmother. Her husband, Hazimanolis Malliarakis, was the one who built the House of the Blue Shutters for Marigo and the one next to it for his other daughter.

When Marigo's sister died without an heir, the house reverted to the family according to the custom, and eventually it was passed down to Eleni. By the time we arrived in Kasos, that house next door had crumbled into ruins. But in Uncle George's childhood it was in perfect condition, inhabited by a couple from Karpathos, whose daughter, a little girl named Evamorphia, was Uncle George's playmate.

There, in the house next door, is where the tale begins. George and Evamorphia used to collect pieces of broken crockery in the abandoned foundations, and pretend they were pieces of money, their value determined by their size. Once George wanted to buy something, and he offered Evamorphia a huge fragment he had unearthed with great care from a foundation.

"I'm sorry, I haven't any change," he said, drawing out the large piece ostentatiously. But if Evamorphia was impressed, she concealed the fact.

"No change?" she said. "Well, give it here. I'll change it for you." With that, she took George's piece of pottery and dropped it on the stones at his feet.

"There you are. There's your change," she said.

Later Old Yia-Yia had a fight with Evamorphia's mother, and she decided that if the family were to live next door, they would have to pay rent. Eleni said that was impossible, these people were her friends. But Old Yia-Yia was intransigent. The rent must be paid. They could not give the house for nothing.

George was inconsolable, sitting on the wall, watching Evamorphia and her parents packing their belongings. But he could not express his sorrow or Old Yia-Yia would have beaten him. (She was a fierce woman who used to beat her grandsons just for amusement.) He kept all his injury inside, but one day it came out unexpectedly. He saw Evamorphia's mother in the street and called out an obscenity to her, as though she, poor woman, were to blame.

Evamorphia's mother replied coolly, with an epigram. "Whatever teacher you sit down with," she said, "that's the lesson you will learn."

And that was very appropriate, for whatever the obscenity had been, George had learned it from Old Yia-Yia. But what George did not know was that the saying held true for grown-ups as well. And it was Old Yia-Yia's mother, the Virago, who had taught her all the curses she would ever need.

Venturing into the house next door, trying to console himself for his loss, George found wedding chests, broken crockery, and *tsimbouks*. These pipes were relics of his great-grandfather's generation, for by the time Old Yia-Yia married, no one smoked *tsimbouks* in Kasos anymore.

They even looked like relics, lying in the bottom of the wedding chest, peaceable remains exhumed on the third anniversary of interment. George was unearthing them decades after the last memorial for Hazimanolis Malliarakis had been sung, almost half a century after the phantoms of the Virago's heart had been laid to rest forever, not by any offering of *kolyva* and honey cakes but by a feast of vengeance.

At once, George imagined them as weapons: long, pointed lances. One by one, he fastened them to the end of a wooden pole and thrust them in desperate, purposeless revenge against the wall of that now forever empty house. His grandmother found him raging like a maddened dwarf, his lance raised against an empty wall, striking at the faceless phantoms of his heart.

She threw up her hands and said, "You hear? You hear?" (She always used this expression to nurse a growing wrath, though in itself it meant nothing.) "What are you doing there?" And George stopped, frozen. Grandmother saw it was a *tsimbouk,* and she said, "Where did you find that?"

George pointed next door, and then his grandmother understood that he had dug it up in the foundation of that house built by her father sometime before he sailed away on his last journey.

Old Yia-Yia told the story to Uncle George, to my father, and her other grandsons, and she repeated it every time they asked her. In 1935, when the family found itself living in Wembley Park in North London, little Marigo, now a woman of ninety-three, was still telling the story.

The Kikos family had a widow sister, and Hazimanolis's brother, named Hazimalliaras, was having an affair with her. Hazi was a prefix added to a Christian name, which indicated—in imitation of

the Moslems who call themselves *Hadji* after they
have made the pilgrimage to Mecca—that the bearer
has made a Christian pilgrimage to Jerusalem and
been baptized in the Jordan River. Thus Hazimanolis'
name meant Manuel The Pilgrim. And Hazimalliaras
was Hazi too, because the relatives and descendants
of pilgrims were also called Hazi. Malliaras itself was
a nickname meaning hairy or hirsute, because he had
thick blond hair and his chest and arms were hairy.

Hazimanolis was afraid that Hazimalliaras would
marry the widow. And as the eldest brother and head
of the family, he felt responsible to put a stop to the
affair. He intervened, not with Hazimalliaras, but
instead with the Kikos family, who owed Hazimanolis
a debt. Hazimanolis threatened that if the widow did
not stop her designs, he would present their promis-
sory note when it fell due and arrest their ship in
payment.

The Kikoses were outraged. In response, they
courted Hazimalliaras more openly than ever. For his
part, Hazimanolis sailed to Alexandria, where the
note had been signed and had to be presented. Thus
it happened that he arrived in Alexandria sometime
around 1850.

The ship was moored in the harbor, and after dinner, Mavrandonis (later Captain Elias's boatswain),
and two other sailors took Hazimanolis ashore in the
lifeboat. The sailors rowed slowly, picking their way
among the gray forms and looming anchor chains for
the fog was so thick you couldn't see your feet.

Mavrandonis sat in the bow, calling out instructions in a voice that must have seemed unusually loud
and clear on a night when you might imagine you

could hear as poorly as you could see. But his voice carried across the harbor, perhaps to the conspirators themselves assembled on shore. And in the stern sat the captain, unbending, resolute, determined on his course.

Hazimanolis must have known what was up as soon as they landed and he stepped on the quay. The spokesman said "Good evening," addressing him in a voice that was unusually composed and dignified considering the errand and the fact that in a fog that thick you would expect a man to shout.

But he didn't shout, this unknown spokesman. He only said, "Good evening, Hazimanolis," a greeting appropriate enough, except that in this case the evening would last for all eternity. At that signal, the forms sprang out all around them.

Hazimanolis must have known who they were and what they intended as soon as he saw the shapes emerging from the darkness. He raised his Malacca walking stick and pulled his two arms asunder, stripping a twenty-five-inch blade. But there was no way he could be quick enough to walk into that ambuscade and survive. An instant later, a man fell on Hazimanolis from the rear and thrust his own pointed and laconic message an inch or two below the captain's neck.

"They've killed your captain," cried a sailor, running past Mavrandonis and the other men waiting at the landing. They ran and found Hazimanolis dead in the street, barely a hundred yards from safety.

At sunrise, the city was revealed like a face before a veil, the rigging of all the Kasiot ships arranged in an insignia of death as unmistakable as a woman's parted hair. The yards were crossed in mourning, black and naked against the sky, including the yards of the Kikos's ship, in a shameless travesty of the custom.

The Kikoses were arrested, for every Kasiot in Alexandria knew the debt they owed the captain and the grudge. A lawyer advised them to nominate one of their kin to confess to the crime. (Under Ottoman law, the only guilty one was the one whose blow caused death.) And that is how they came to nominate not the murderer himself, but his younger brother Basil.

They expected him to spend a month or two in prison and then be set free. And they chose Basil because, unlike the guilty one, he was unmarried and so would not temporarily deprive a wife and children of a livelihood.

Meanwhile, Old Yia-Yia's mother, the Virago, arrived in Alexandria with her children and the maids, like country relatives in town for a cousin's wedding. There was an air of anticipation about her, a certain eagerness for events to come that was inappropriate in a mourning widow.

The Khedive, or ruler of Egypt, was in Alexandria then, listening to his subjects' grievances. Late one afternoon, in the audience hall with the Moorish portals, he was about to hear one more case. The guards had stepped inside to receive his instructions and the door was left ajar. That moment, a little girl padded across the marble floor, as directly as she pads into her story: Old Yia-Yia, at the age of eight.

"Who is this pretty child?" asked the Khedive.

"Who is this pretty child?" said Uncle George,

quoting both the Khedive and his grandmother, as he retold the story a century later. "Who is she and what does she want?"

The guards told him that she was the daughter of a Greek woman waiting outside, who demanded retribution for her husband's murder.

"Let her enter," replied the Khedive in his kindly voice. "Hers is the last case we shall hear today."

The Khedive had been told that the confessed murderer was really innocent, and his response to the Virago was a masterpiece of conciliation.

"The Khedive suggests," an interpreter translated, "that we wait until this pretty girl is grown to be a woman. Then she can tell us whether the defendant should be punished."

But the Virago's reply made the smile vanish from the Khedive's face. "Rather than agree to such a thing," she said, "I would have my daughter's throat cut before my eyes and never see her grow to be a woman."

Now Basil's fate began to darken. The lawyer tried a different tack. He claimed that because the defendant was a Turkish subject, he must be tried in Rhodes, in the court that had jurisdiction over Kasos. The lawyer hoped the Virago would not be able to afford more transportation and hotel bills and would have to give up pursuit.

But he underestimated her. She had spent all her dowry, and now she appealed to the Malliarakis family to save their honor. They provided money (ruining themselves in the process), and with their assistance, the Virago and her brood of plaintiffs journeyed on to Rhodes.

The trial did not take long: Basil was found guilty by his own confession. But the Rhodian judges were no more eager to have him executed than the Khedive had been. They invoked a law, providing that if any member of the plaintiff's family grant mercy to the accused, his sentence would be commuted and his life spared.

The judges ordered the Virago to bring the children to the execution. Let them stand with her below the scaffold, and if the head of this innocent man was to roll tomorrow, then the children would be there to see it roll. Unless she wished to spare them the horror of such a sight and grant him mercy now herself. Would she grant him mercy?

"I grant him nothing," the Virago said, "and neither will my children."

"Then a good night to you," the judges answered, "and a good night to your children."

Everyone went away to prepare for the next day, the Virago and her children to their lodgings, the Kikos brothers and the lawyers to visit Basil in the dungeon. The Virago gave her children their final coaching, saying, "He will ask you to spare his life. But whatever he says, you are not to speak to him. They will show you the sword they will use to cut off his head, and if you say a word, they will use that blade to cut off your heads instead."

In the dungeon, the lawyer said to Basil, "The children will be the ones to save you. You must kneel down before them until one of them grants you mercy. That way your life will be spared."

And Basil Kikos listened to his instructions in a kind of daze, for still he did not comprehend the danger he was in. He had agreed to confess to the crime if his brothers and the lawyer would secure his freedom. He had done his part; the rest he left to them.

As for the guilty brother, we can suppose if the man had been anywhere on earth that night, he was in Basil's prison cell. Maybe he was sitting on a stool the obliging Turks had brought for him, unable to look at Basil or any of the others in the eye. In the meantime, in the city square, the attendants were putting up the scaffold where the whole population of the city would gather the next day.

Basil came out of prison, like a Christian thrown to the lions. The square was full of people—Greeks, Turks, and Jews—surrounding the scaffold like the sea. Basil was led up the steps. Then, in front of priests, judges, dignitaries of the Rhodian government, and almost the entire population of the city, the Virago challenged him.

"You hear? You hear?" she cried. "You hear? You hear? There goes the foul cowardly villain."

"Old harlot," Basil called to her. "When I am free, I will tie you in a foresail and throw you to the bottom of the sea so the sun will never shine on you."

"Blaspheming villain," the Virago replied. "May the plague take you and all your kinsmen. May they all follow you in a procession to the grave. May your mother kiss their foreheads in the casket after yours. For you won't go free except into your grave."

"Vile slattern," Kikos returned, groping for words to answer her, "may they take all your children away on the sheet. May they . . ."

But the widow bested him.

"The same to you and all who love you," she cried. "May your mother curse the day you were conceived. May the womb that carried you be eaten by the pox. And may the hand that cut your birth cord burn in hell."

Basil Kikos turned away defeated, outdone in cursing by the Virago. That moment he saw two priests standing on the scaffold, darkening the platform like shadows. Soundlessly, they moved toward him, one holding a gilded Bible, the other a spoon and a chalice.

Basil shrank from them and an instant later he received a second shock. Behind the priests there were two more figures in black hoods, holding up the instruments of another calling: one the short, pointed sword, the other the long, curved, glistening one.

He stumbled backward down the steps, almost into the Virago's arms.

"The children! The children!" shouted his brothers from the crowd. Basil remembered the instructions he had heard so often, and at last he understood them. In an instant, he forgot all the threats and curses he had heaped upon this family.

"Little boy," he said, to the first of the Virago's children, "have mercy on me."

But the little boy did not have mercy, or at least he did not show it, and Basil proceeded to the next child.

"Have mercy on me, my child," he begged him, but this child was silent too.

Basil proceeded down the line of children, that family phalanx, a solid chain forged of common fear:

six terror-stricken children bound to silence. From one to the other, Basil crawled on his hands and knees.

And in his frenzy he made it easier for them than it might have been. No sooner had one child refused him than he crawled on, desperately, to the next child. In that way, he wasted them. In an instant, five were lost forever. Between him and death was a final child: a girl of eight.

With this one, he took more time.

"What's her name?" he cried to the onlookers standing by.

"I wasn't the one who told him," said Old Yia-Yia, more than half a century later. "I was so frightened I couldn't speak."

"Who it was we shall never know," said Uncle George, after another half a century. "Perhaps the lawyer or one of the Kikos brothers."

But I believe the Virago told him. Why would she not have responded to the question as any other mother, identified her child before the stranger, even straightened her hair a little?!

"What's her name?" cried Basil Kikos. "Will someone tell me this child's name?"

"Marigo," the Virago said.

"Save me, Marigo," cried Basil. "Have mercy on me, and I shall do your bidding for the rest of my life!"

But Marigo did not have mercy. A look from her mother quenched all mercy in her.

"Save me, Marigo," cried Basil again. "Grant mercy to me, and I will crawl ahead of you the rest of my days and sweep the earth beneath your feet."

"We grant you nothing, you worthless faggot,"

the Virago said, and Basil Kikos turned away, put down again.

"The sword! The sword!" the judges cried. "Children, unless you have mercy on this man, they will use this sword to cut off his head!"

And they passed the broad, curved, glistening blade before each one of the children, those diminutive accomplices of the widow's vengeance.

The children were paralyzed with fear, unable to look at each other, or at anyone else. They could see nothing except this huge glistening blade. But still they did not grant mercy, and the guards passed the blade to the Virago. Because she had ordered that feast of vengeance, it was only fitting that she approve it.

That was the incident her great-grandson mentioned at the cocktail party, when she lifted the sword to her enraptured lips. But she lifted it before the execution, not afterward, and the only outrage she committed was against religion, not against nature.

"Blessed be this sword that brings me vengeance," she said, and kissed it as though it were an icon. Then, returning the sword to the executioners, she made the sign of the cross and folded her hands upon her breast.

Two guards at Basil's either arm led him back up the stairs to the scaffold. The priests advanced from opposite directions, one holding the gilded Bible, the other the chalice and the spoon. For a moment, Basil must have stopped his struggling to watch them. He must have watched the priest raise the chalice and extend the spoon toward him.

For a single moment, Basil Kikos opened his mouth in that gesture of acceptance he had first made when he was a baby in his mother's arms. As the priest tipped the spoon upon his tongue, he had just enough time to wonder why they were giving him Communion, there on the scaffold where he was supposed to die.

Then the next moment the truth was in him: truth bursting out of mystery. With the Blood of his Redeemer in his mouth, he knew the truth. His mouth was full of it, and he tasted the death in it, not the Eternal Life.

For the first time he knew he was going to die. As the two priests hovered in solicitation for his soul, crossing themselves and moaning a litany for the dead, Basil cried out like a damned soul in descent to hell, and spit the Blood of his Redeemer from his mouth.

After that the executioners knew they must be swift. The priests hurried away in horror. In their places, the other two advanced, converging from two directions, hooded like the fates.

For a while Basil fought them cleverly. If design had deserted him before, it came to him now, in the desperate instinct of a surrounded animal. He knew the swing of the giant blade would have to catch him neatly on the neck, so he did not try to evade those two messengers of doom. Instead, he waited with his shoulders hunched, his neck buried between them. He crouched in the center of the platform, like an owl, like a bird of darkness, his steely eyes blinking in the face of danger.

But the executioners had hunted many men before him and were familiar with such wiles. One raised the huge, curved blade; and as Basil had predicted, he could not find the two or three inches of flesh to make the clean cut. The blade was still poised in the air, hovering. In the meantime, working with his partner, the second celebrant poked Basil in the ribs with the pointed sword, drawing blood, then fell flat against the floor.

Basil shuddered with the pain. His back arched, his head popped up from between his shoulders, and his neck elongated. That instant, the second dancer did his pirouette, with the long, curved, glistening blade. From where he lay safely against the platform, the first executioner saw the blade complete one enormous, glittering arc against the sky. Then, the next instant, on the planking of the scaffold fell Basil Kikos's head.

"Come quickly, Elias, I found the Virago," called Uncle George, one evening in Kasos. I hurried to his room, expecting to find another effigy of evil, but instead I found a dignified portrait of some members of the Malliarakis family: several tall men in high collars and well-clipped beards. Sitting among them was as kindly a Kasiot mother as I have ever seen. She was a small woman, in the black of mourning, with a peaceful face, soft eyes, and, on her lap, a pair of folded knobby hands.

"Not very fierce for a virago," I said.

"She wasn't fierce. Except for what happened on the square in Rhodes, she never committed any violence in her life."

Then it must have been a dream, coming on her as suddenly as any other dream (only in this case it lasted for a year), and left her when it passed from her, as cleansed of terror and compulsion as anyone on waking.

There is one more episode to be reported before we lay the Virago to her rest. In 1911, Uncle George went to visit Old Yia-Yia in Alexandria. The Virago had been dead for many years, and little Marigo had become a grandmother many times. Always hot-tempered and meddling, she had quarreled with relatives in Syros and departed in a fury for Alexandria on the pretext of visiting her sons.

When he arrived, Uncle George was told Old Yia-Yia was not at home. She had gone to Port Said to sing dirges by the coffin of a Kasiot gentleman. A Mr. Kikos, by name.

The deceased was a son of one of Basil's brothers, maybe the son of the murderer himself. The ceremony in Rhodes had been concluded and now, sixty years later, there was this new ceremony to take its place.

This latest Mr. Kikos had gone to meet his Maker, and little Marigo, who had denied mercy to the ancestor, hurried off to sing dirges for the descendant. Having attended one ceremony at the age of eight, Old Yia-Yia was at it again at sixty-eight.

"Oh, Mr. Kikos, black blood is flowing from my heart for you. Oh, Mr. Kikos, bitter was your Communion."

The author at sea. Photo by Robert McCabe.

BEGGING YOUR PARDON, ANOTHER VENGEANCE

I have always been confused by all the Turkish coins in use in Kasos: piastres, paras, mezitia. Once during our stay, I asked Uncle George to explain them.

"Let's see," he said. "The Turkish pound was worth a hundred piastres. And the meziti was worth twenty piastres. There were smaller coins called kartakia and octarakia. And then there was an even smaller coin called . . . an even smaller coin called . . ."

His eyes were lifted to the ceiling.

"The metalik! I remember, the metalik."

"How many piastres to the metalik?"

"None. The metalik was smaller than a piastre. One piastre was worth four metaliks. Then there was another subdivision of the piastre called a para."

"What was a para?"

"A fortieth of a piastre. Every piastre was worth forty paras, but the metalik was independent of the para, and its value varied from place to place. When I said the piastre was worth four metaliks, I meant only in Constantinople. In Salonika, the piastre might be worth 3.5 metaliks, in Beirut 3.25, in Smyrna 3."

"Good God."

"So now do you understand Turkish money?"

"I understand why the Ottoman Empire col-lapsed."

"Now, by the way, I'll tell you something else the Virago did in Rhodes, and to understand the story, all you have to remember is that there were forty paras to the piastre."

"Forty paras to the piastre."

"The Virago had taken all her children to the café, with a maid who was accompanying them, an earlier version of Aphrodite named Artemia. Suddenly, the Virago had a craving for eggplants, and she told Artemia to get some from the greengrocer. The Virago knew that in Rhodes, the eggplants grew to be very long—very long indeed—one foot long . . ."

"I beg your pardon."

"The eggplants grew to be very long, as they still do, one foot long . . . Oh yes, of course, excuse me! The eggplants—begging your pardon—grew to be very long. By your indulgence, they were one foot long. And very tender."

And so, with apologies, Uncle George told of the Virago's craving for eggplants, and the satisfaction of that craving in—begging your pardon—another vengeance.

"How many shall I get?" said Artemia.

"Oh, one piastre's worth," said the Virago, and she gave Artemia a piastre. Now the Virago was reckoning on the price in Kasos. Even today, Kasos produces no vegetables at all, and very little fruit, only a few grapes and figs. Vegetables have to be imported from Rhodes or Karpathos, and the price includes the transportation. But in Rhodes the land is very fertile, and fruit and vegetables are abundant, and the eggplants—begging your pardon—are very long and tender. So Artemia went off to the greengrocer with her piastre for the eggplants.

"How many do you want?" said the greengrocer.

"One piastre's worth," said Artemia.

"One piastre's worth?"

"That's right."

"In that case," said the greengrocer, "open your arms."

Artemia opened her arms, and the greengrocer laid the eggplants across, very long eggplants, very long and tender. How many eggplants in Artemia's arms? Forty! In Rhodes, eggplants cost one para each, and there were forty paras in the piastre. Forty eggplants in Artemia's arms!

She came back to the café carrying the eggplants like firewood, hardly able to see over the top. And when the Virago saw her coming, she said, "What evil is this?" and Artemia said, "Didn't you tell me to buy one piastre's worth of eggplants? Here they are, one piastre's worth, forty eggplants."

And with that, the Virago picked up one of the forty eggplants—a very ripe and tender one—and hit Artemia on the head.

Elias of George, called Kulukundis. (Elias of the Fez)
c. 1832.

THE SONG OF ELIAS GEORGE

*I*n Kasos, parents were not free to name their children. Instead, Kasiot custom chose the infant for the name. I am Elias because I am a first son, and my father's father was also a first son and my grandfather's grandfather, that original first son, was also Elias Kulukundis.

That first Elias, the first Kulukundis of record, wore the fez and baggy trousers of the Aegean Islands. He named his first son George, after his father. And when this second George became a father, his own firstborn was Elias again, for *his* father. That was Captain Elias, who shared the house of the blue shutters with his wife, Eleni.

When Eleni bore a son, that latest firstborn was named George again: Uncle George of the bananas and the plaster cats. And when Uncle George became a father, and his brothers Nicholas, Manuel, John, and Michael all had children, their first sons were named Elias again, resulting in the proliferation of Eliases we have in the Kulukundis family.

Though the custom of naming the first son after the father was widespread all over Greece, customs have varied greatly in the naming of the other children. In Kasos, the second son was named for the mother's father, the third son for the father's eldest brother, the fourth for the mother's, and so on.

The daughters followed the same pattern, in reverse. The first daughter was named for the mother's mother, the second for the father's, the third for the mother's eldest sister, and so on. My family tree provides numerous examples of the male naming patterns, but few of the female. That is because the old Kulukundis fathers were very good at getting their way in the lottery of the genders, and sons were always preferred.

"How many children do you have?" someone might ask a Kasiot father.

"Four," the father might reply, "four children and two daughters."

The naming customs were directly related to inheritance. A parent was free to pass on all property acquired in his lifetime according to his will, and he would usually distribute it equally among all his children. But what property the parent had in turn inherited, the *ancestral* property, had to follow a code that was parallel to the naming customs.

A first son inherited the property of his father's father, whose name he bore. A first daughter would inherit all her mother's ancestral property, including her mother's house. In Kasos houses were owned maternally, and when a man married, he went to live in his wife's house.

This custom had the effect of removing the necessity of human choice. Only a very wealthy man could afford to build a house for each of several daughters, but in any family there was already at least one house, the mother's. Without the custom, the family would find it difficult to decide which daughter should have it. What mortal could confer the joys of wedlock on one girl and deny them to another?

But the custom decided the question without controversy. The first daughter would have it, and all her unmarriageable sisters could live with her, like my aunts in Syros, as a retinue of attendant maidens. The elder sister did not seek the privilege, and her parents did not confer it on her. It simply fell to her in the way the universe was ordered, by an inexorable tradition, in the lottery of birth.

The customs are older than the Venetians and probably originated in the religion of ancient Greece. There too a first son was named for his father's father. After the father's death, this first son would tend his grave and perform services in ministration for his soul. For this reason, by religious precept, the son would acquire the land adjacent to his father's grave, which would then become his ancestral property, to be handed on to his own first son.

But the names are more than a custom; they are a manifestation of eternity. The child is not simply named for his grandfather. To those black-cowled seers of the island, he *is* the grandfather incarnate.

"The eyes," says one.

"The mouth," another.

"The forehead," a third, in chorus.

"Captain Stathe!" called my aunts in Syros to a

twelve year-old boy in a T-shirt with RYE across his chest. In those aged women's minds, this boy was Captain Stathe, their niece's husband, who built the villa in the hills and died in 1942, the year of my brother's birth.

Stathe is Captain Stathe, I am Captain Elias, and my cousin Eleni, the younger of twin girls, an American woman who teaches remedial reading on New York's Lower East Side, is the mistress of the house of the blue shutters. We are all our grandparents.

As long as there was an Elias George born in London in 1932, then five generations earlier we could assume an earlier one. And the first one in turn foretells the second, for as long as there was a first Elias George in Kasos in 1824, five generations later, wherever he might find himself, there would be another, providing that in the span of those several generations, the seeds of three firstborns would endure, each filling his portion of the hiatus.

The equation, therefore, stretches further than even birth or death. The two Eliases do not postdate or antedate each other except in time, which is irrelevant. As each time-imprisoned father, each poor impassioned George Elias or Elias George, performed his rhythm of paternity, there was a song of generations sounding in his ears, a song to sing a coming son, coaxing him to conception from the void.

In that insistent relation of conceiver to conceived, the father began not to know if he was the father or the son, not to know who was coming and who would come, until finally, as the rhythm increased and the song was deepened, father and son had both escaped, leapt out of time.

Now, as the space between them widened and receded, they became not only father and son but also grandfather and grandson, withdrawing outward, returning inward once again, until finally at the climax both of the rhythm and of the song, they were just one person in a timeless silence, singing what started as a song of generations and became the music of eternity, a song that has no beginning and no end: Elias George, George Elias, Elias George, George Elias George Elias George Elias George.

Sisters of the author's maternal grandmother. The inspiration for "The Unknown God."

THE UNKNOWN GOD

A young girl prepared a mystic altar to an Unknown God," Uncle George said. "She worshiped him ahead of time, and when he came, she loved him and was devoted to him all her life."

The way a Kasiot marriage was arranged, the girl might be walking on the square in Phry, arm in arm with girlfriends. In her courtyard, her father and her uncles might be talking to another father and other uncles. And by the time the young girl came home, the partner of her life would have been chosen for her and the day of her wedding would be set.

Until then, as my uncle said, she must keep an altar to an Unknown God. From earliest childhood, she believed there was one man destined to come for her. His coming had been foreknown on the seventh evening of her life, at the "ceremony of the seven," when as an infant in her cradle she had lain in dreamless sleep while three women of antiquity hovered over her.

They were the three Fates, one with a spindle and thread to spin out the infant's time on earth, the second with a scissors to cut it off at the appointed place, the third with an open ledger in which to write the infant's life. Throughout her girlhood, she might pray to that ancient trinity, begging them for revelation. But the three stern women kept their secret, remaining deaf to the prayers of a maiden's heart.

Once a year, each June on the feast of Kleithona, if a girl was virtuous and faithfully performed a ritual, she might be granted a vision of her future husband. The night before, a young boy would draw water from the cistern in the house of a newly married bride. In doing so, he could not speak, not even if someone spoke to him.

"Don't say a word," hissed black-cowled maidens. "In the name of the Virgin, keep a cross upon your lips."

In silence, the young boy would fill the barrel with water from the cistern and with the help of these maidens, he would set the barrel on the roof. The women would cover the barrel with a red handkerchief and seal it with a padlock to keep the potion pure. Now the water was "speechless water," possessed of magic powers. All night, it would sit on the housetop where the stars could see it and impregnate it with their powers of augury.

The next morning, on the feast of Kleithona, all the unmarried girls of the village would gather at this house of the newly married bride. Accompanied by mothers, aunts, and cousins, they would make a circle in the courtyard, and the barrel of water would be brought down and set in the middle. Each unmarried girl would bring a ripened fruit, a pear or peach or pomegranate. She would pin a piece of jewelry in it so that it could be identified as hers, and put it in the water.

A virtuous girl, one whose father and mother both were living, would be chosen to sit beside the barrel. Then the *mandinadhas* would begin. Around the circle, a low poetic murmuring would proceed, as each venerable muse would deliver a couplet of her family.

"Your body is a minaret,
Your shadow is a garden.
And all the moisture on your brow,
Is perfume from Arabia."

As soon as the *mandinadha* was recited, the virtuous girl would thrust down her virgin hand and draw out a peach or a pomegranate to see whose it would be.

"My Kyrenia's!" cried a mother, recognizing a filigree earring or an Austrian coin in the fruit. All her friends would scream with pleasure, and Kyrenia would blush and keep her eyes on the pebbled courtyard floor. For she was the one whose body was a minaret, whose shadow was a garden, and the moisture of whose brow was perfume from Arabia.

One by one, the elder women sang their couplets, and one by one the fruits of the maidens were drawn from the speechless water by the virtuous girl presiding at the rim. Finally, each girl learned something either of herself or of her future husband, and blushed at the announcement, however inconclusive it might be.

Each girl would then take home a glassful of the speechless water, the potion fructified by the bejeweled fruits of every maiden in the village. And that night, before she went to bed, she would go out into her courtyard with a red ribbon tied around her waist. She would take a mouthful of the water and two handfuls of barley.

Wearing her nightgown, with the red ribbon around her waist, she would turn around in the center of the courtyard, lightly as a Nereid. With both hands full of barley and a sip of speechless water unswallowed in her mouth, she would turn faster and faster, her arms stretched out like the blades of a windmill.

Turning as fast as she could go, she would open her fists so the barley flew out and scattered against the courtyard walls. Next she would go to her room, drink down the rest of the speechless water, and have a little wine and a salt *koulouri* to disturb her sleep. (A *koulouri* is a dry Kasiot doughnut made of barley flour.) Then, with the red ribbon still around her waist, she would get into bed, and as she set her head against the pillow, she would murmur this prayer to the three black-shrouded women of antiquity:

"In Hades my Fates are dancing,
And the Fate of my Fates,
And if she is sitting let her stand,
And if she is standing let her come
And bring me a dream this night
Of the man I'm to marry."

That night, if the girl was virtuous, the Fates would hear her prayer. In her sleep, her Unknown God would come to her. He might be someone she knew or he might be a stranger. But whoever he was, she would not be afraid as he bent over her, for he would be smiling in a kindly way and she would know he was the man she would belong to for the rest of her life.

He would take her by the red ribbon around her waist, and she would feel herself drawn toward him by a power beyond herself. She would see his face, smiling at her, and she would hear his whispering voice, as soft as milk: "Let us go together now and reap the harvest you have sown."

The next day, in the courtyards of the island, each girl proclaimed her vision, according to the custom.

"I saw him."

"Did you? And what did he do?"

"He stood over me, at the foot of my bed."

"And then?"

"He bent over me, and drew me to him by the red cord around my waist."

"And then?"

"He said, 'Let us go together now and reap the harvest you have sown.' "

"And then?"

"I don't know . . . nothing."

"Nothing?"

"There isn't any more, is there? I mean . . . I don't remember."

Every girl had seen exactly what the custom ordained, nothing more or less. Each girl doubted the visions of the others and became angry when she in turn was doubted. But no matter how faithfully the girls performed the ritual, there was no certainty or conviction in any of them.

And then a Kasiot girl saw something different, and among the maidens of the island, that vision became a legend.

The girl was named Katina, and she lived in a white gypsum fortress near the top of the town of Poli, high on a hill among the surrounding mountains.

That year her older sister Sofia had been married.

Sofia's husband was a captain who lived in Syros, and after she married, Sofia had gone to live on that island, two hundred miles away. They were only visiting in Kasos, on their way to Alexandria. The captain's ship was anchored in the lee of Makra Island, and they were staying a few days at Sofia's house.

Katina usually slept in the *moussandra,* a little attic above a ladder and a trapdoor, where her mother and father used to sleep. Her father had died several years before, and now Katina slept in the *moussandra* herself. She liked it because it was far away from where everyone else was sleeping, and when the trapdoor was closed, her mother couldn't hear her and didn't know what time she went to sleep. But when Sofia and her husband came home to visit, their mother decided that they should sleep in the *moussandra.*

"They need a quieter place to sleep," she explained, so Katina gave up her room and took her clothes and things to a little alcove off the living room where the maid Maria usually slept.

Katina didn't mind doing a favor for her older sister, but that was before she realized how proud and boastful Sofia had become. Ever since her wedding, Sofia pretended to be superior just because she was married.

Syros was not like Kasos at all, she said. It was a big city, where ships came from all over the world, and it had a big square, where hundreds of people walked back and forth at night. In Syros, Sofia explained, you didn't say good evening to everyone the way you did in Kasos, only to people you knew, otherwise people would think you had no upbringing.

Katina hated the way everyone had to make a fuss over her sister just because she was married. When the speechless water was taken down from the roof, Sofia was the only woman in the village not to sit on a cushion on the courtyard floor and sing the *mandinadhas*. She sat in an armchair on the upper terrace, beside the captain, looking down at everyone, as though she were not part of the ceremony at all.

Her husband was a great deal older than Sofia, supposed to be very intelligent, though Katina had never heard him say anything except, "The weather in Kasos is truly magnificent, let us thank God for such a glorious day!" They sat in their armchairs on the upper terrace like a king and queen, and after each *mandinadha,* Sofia would glance at her husband, pulling gravely on his pipe, and she would catch his eye and smile at him.

Katina began to resent her older sister, and once she spoke to her about it openly.

"Why do you make fun of everything on Kasos?" she asked her. "What do you find funny about the feast of Kleithona? Don't you believe in it at all?"

"I did once," Sofia said, rippling with laughter. "But now why should I, now that I'm married?"

And with that, Sofia swaggered off to the quiet bedroom, leaving Katina to wipe away her tears of anger.

That night, Katina put on her nightgown, tied the red ribbon round her waist, and took two handfuls of barley and a sip of speechless water. In the center of the courtyard, her cheeks still burning with her sister's laughter, she whirled as fast as a dervish and scattered her barley to the four winds. Later, as she set her head against the pillow, she prayed to the Fates, as fervently as anyone had ever prayed to any god in the Pantheon of the islands.

And Katina truly must have been a virtuous girl, for her prayers were answered. Hardly had an hour passed since she drank the Karpathian wine and ate the salt *koulouri* when the god himself appeared to her, not in a dream as he appeared to other girls, but incarnate, a word become flesh.

She was lying awake, her face to the wall. Her eyes were tracing the curls and windings of a panel below the ceiling. Suddenly, she became aware that the room was glowing with an unknown light. At first she thought it was the votive candles before the icons. But the icons were beyond the screen in the living room and this light was in the alcove itself, growing steadily brighter, like the flame in a kerosene lantern when you raise the wick.

She turned, and suddenly she saw a man's head and shoulders framed in the window, with a candle held before his face. In that one instant, she saw him perfectly, his face silent as an icon, the candlelight around his head like the halo of an archangel. She sat up in bed; she couldn't help giving a tiny cry of fright; and with that, the candle streaked away in an instant, like a falling star.

The man vanished as suddenly as he appeared, and that window of her future, so miraculously illuminated, was darkened once again, enclosing nothing but a branch of bougainvillea and a patch of moonless sky.

The next morning, Katina announced her vision to her girlfriends.

"I saw him."

"Did you? What happened?"

"He stood outside my window, holding a candle to light his way."

"He *did?*" cried one of the girls. "Is that what you dreamed?"

"I didn't dream it," Katina said. "I saw him. I was still awake when he came and stood at the window by my bed and held a candle to light his way."

"Impossible," said another girl, astounded. "No one has ever dreamed of that before."

"I don't care what other people dream," Katina said. "I actually saw him. He was standing at the window by my bed."

"It cannot be," murmured a dozen voices, but without conviction. The idea had begun to grow on them that it might be possible. And if it was, these girls were thinking for the first time, then it absolutely wouldn't matter what anyone had dreamed before.

But for every visionary there are seven skeptics. That is not a Kasiot saying, but it ought to be. Living near Katina and her mother in the white gypsum fortress were seven sisters of Katina's grandmother: seven black-cowled maidens who had ruled that threshold since anyone could remember. When their older sister married, they had accompanied the newly married couple in a solemn procession as inevitably as the trousseau or dowry.

They lived there long after their Pure Monday, the first day of Lent when urchins of the village attached padlocks to the doors of all conspicuously unmarried women, signifying that their time of marriage was locked away. On that threshold, they became an eternal seven, ushering in all arrivals and departures there.

Sofia brought them out into the courtyard, as she was now the one to resent her sister's sudden popularity. Sofia reasoned that if anyone would be inclined to mistrust Katina's vision, it would be these ladies, seven maidens who in seven decades had received no gods of any sort, not even in their dreams.

One by one, Sofia routed them out of the cracks and crevices where they lived, two from the cookhouse, two more from another little house, three more from the storeroom where the grain and vegetables were kept. Out they came in order of seniority: Anezoulla, Erinoulla, Evdoukoulla, Marigoulla, Zografoulla, Mangafoulla, and Mertianoulla. Tapping their canes and shuffling their slippers on the pebbled floor, they reclaimed their dominion of the courtyard.

"Katina saw her future husband!" announced the girls of Poli with one voice. "Not in a dream. But standing at the window by her bed!"

"Indeed?" said Anezoulla, in her cackling voice.

"Impossible," said Erinoulla, in hers.

"She only dreamed of him," said Evdoukoulla, Marigoulla, and Zografoulla, at the same time.

"She only thought she saw him," said Mangafoulla and Mertianoulla.

"No, she saw him! She saw him!" cried all the girls of Poli.

"All right, in that case," said Anezoulla, raising her cane, "out of here, all of you." And with that, the court of inquiry was cleared of any maiden under sixty, except for the defendant.

Seven black-robed judges brought Katina before
their inquisitorial stools. Meanwhile, banished from
the courtyards, the girls of Poli peeped silently above
the walls.

"In your own words, child," said Anezoulla, in a
voice that was all patience and condescension, "tell
us what happened."

"I was trying to go to sleep," Katina said, "when
suddenly I saw a light in the room, and I turned over
to see who was there, and then I saw my future husband standing in the window."

"What did he look like?"

"I couldn't see his face, because he was holding a
candle right in front of it. I was frightened and I cried
out, and then suddenly he disappeared."

A murmur passed around that shrouded crescent.
Adjusting their hoods of office, the judges resumed
their inquiry.

"In your own words, child," said Erinoulla, imi-
tating her sister. "Earlier last night, did you do everything according to the custom?"

Katina nodded.

"What did you do?"

"I spread the barley seed to the four winds, and
I put the red ribbon around my waist, and then I went
to bed."

"And then?"

"And then I drank the rest of the speechless water
and a glass of wine and I ate a salt *koulouri* and
then . . ."

"And then you went to sleep," said Evdokoulla
suddenly.

"That's right."

"Aha! Aha!" cried the black inquisitor, shaking her stick. "You see? You went to sleep, and in your *sleep* the man appeared to you."

"No! No!" Katina said. "I didn't go to sleep, I went to *bed,* and I lay awake for maybe an hour or so, and then I saw him in the window."

"How do you know it wasn't a dream?"

"Because I wasn't asleep. You cannot dream if you aren't asleep."

Another murmur passed around the circle. On the ramparts of the courtyard, the girls of Poli chattered happily.

"Silence!" cried Anezoulla, raising a slipper. Instantly a dozen faces sank below the courtyard wall.

Turning back to the defendant, Anezoulla tried another approach.

"Tell us child," she said. "Did you pray to the Fates, according to the custom?"

"I did."

"And what did you say?"

"I said the prayer I had learned."

"Yes, but what was it? What are the words?"

Katina said the prayer, her hands twisting behind her back just as they did in school when she had to stand up before the whole class and recite the "Our Father." But she got through it without a mistake.

"Just a moment! What did you say, child?" said Anezoulla. "Say those last four lines again."

"And if she is sitting let her stand,
And if she is standing let her come
And bring me a dream this night
Of the man I'm to marry."

"And bring you a *dream* of the man you're to

marry. And bring you a *dream* of him, my child. You asked the Fates to make you dream of him, and that is just what they did. You went to sleep and *dreamed* you saw the man you're going to marry."

"Oh, you don't *want* to believe me," cried Katina with tears in her eyes.

"There, there, it doesn't matter," said Mertianoulla, the youngest sister, putting her arms around Katina. "If you dreamed of him, it's all the same. If you dreamed of the man you're going to marry, you're a very lucky girl."

"That's right," said Mangafoulla. "You dreamed of the man you're going to marry. What more can you ask for?"

Katina stopped crying. Around the courtroom, the shrouded judges watched her. At the walls, the girls of Poli waited, to see if Katina would go back on what she said.

But she did not. The maid did not recant. The maid was obdurate. She wiped her eyes, and in a cool voice, confirmed in heresy, she said, "I did not *dream* of him. I was awake when he came to me, and I saw him with my own eyes."

Now Katina's doom was sealed. Not even kindly Mertianoulla could save her now. Anezoulla rose off her stool, pointing a bony finger. Around her, a final time, judges adjusted their hoods of office.

"Tell me, child," said Anezoulla, "did he speak to you, this man?"

Katina shook her head.

"He didn't say anything?"

"No."

"That is very strange, child," said Anezoulla,

smiling so cunningly now that Katina began to feel uneasy.

"Very strange indeed, since it has been known for generations that on the eve of Kleithona, a young maiden is visited in her sleep by the man she will marry, and he draws her to him by the red cord around her waist and says to her in a voice as soft as milk: 'Let us go together now and reap the harvest you have sown.' You remember that, my child?"

Katina nodded.

"But he didn't say that to you?"

Katina shook her head.

"I wonder if you can explain that, child. Can you tell us why he didn't speak to you?"

Anezoulla waited, her arms folded in her black sleeves. Around her, the judges waited. On the parapets, the girls of Poli waited. But a dreadful silence had fallen on the courtyard. The maid of Poli said nothing.

"Well, perhaps *I* can explain it to *you*," said Anezoulla. "If you had told us that you went to sleep last night and *dreamed* that your future husband stood over you and drew you to him and spoke to you in a voice as soft as milk, we would have believed you. Many girls on the island have dreamed the same. But you tell us that you were not asleep, that you saw him with your own eyes. And that, of course, is the answer. That's the reason he didn't speak to you."

Six judges looked at Anezoulla, wondering what she had in mind.

"What do you mean?" said Katina.

"According to the custom of the island, a girl must be asleep when her future husband comes by her bed. When your future husband came to draw you toward him by the red cord of maidenhood around your waist, he should have found you with your eyes closed, seeing him in your dreams. But instead, he found you awake, as you admit. You sat up in bed and screamed at him. And he must have thought, 'What kind of girl is this? She is supposed to be asleep, but she sits up in bed and screams. No, this girl I do not want for a wife. I will go away and find another girl.' "

And at this devious reasoning, the solemn court of inquiry started cackling and hissing. Seven judges trembled in toothless laughter.

Katina's face was burning with shame and anger. Tears were streaming down her cheeks. There was nothing she could do, nothing she could say to these seven wicked judges, rocking on their stools. Even her companions on the parapets could not help her now.

She ran to her room and lay down on her bed behind the screen, the only place where she could be alone. And beside the vacant window and the bougainvillea, she wept tears of loneliness. Anezoulla's dry cackling laughter came back to her. Why hadn't her future husband spoken? Could it be true that he had gone away, and there would be no husband for her?

Katina thought there could be no other explanation. All her friends would marry, one by one. Only she would be left alone. A Pure Monday would come when she would awake to find a padlock fastened to her door, and all the urchins of the island laughing at her.

Lonely and despairing, Katina wept herself to sleep, praying to the Fates to give her some sign to prove that it wasn't true what her aunt had said, that she wouldn't have a husband. And the Fates heard her prayer and answered it.

Once again, she knew it was not a dream. She woke up on her lonely cot, the tears flowing again as soon as she remembered. She got up and went to the window, and looked out into the little garden at the rear of the house where the bougainvillea was blooming, wine-red against the gypsum walls. And there, through her tears, Katina caught sight of something on the pebbled courtyard floor.

She ran outside to have a closer look, and on the pebbles she saw a neat red spot. It had flowed down neatly over three pebbles, settling into the cracks among them, so that they looked like tiny eggs, dyed red for Easter. And now Katina had her sign, evidence to prove her aunt was wrong. Dried and clinging to the pebbles beneath her window was a patch of red wax: the drippings of the candle the Unknown God had held.

"You see! You see!" Katina cried, though there was no one there to see. Before the shuttered windows, where the seven judges had crawled off into their shady cracks to doze away the hours of the afternoon, Katina danced and shouted, "Come and see! Come and see!"

One by one, the seven guardians came out, two from the cookhouse, two more from the other little house, another three from the storeroom where the dried fruits and vegetables were kept. Out they came, the hobbling storm-troops for moral emergency.

"You see! You see!" cried Katina, dancing and shouting.

"Kyrie Eleison," said Anezoulla, making the sign of the cross. "God the Father protect us!"

"And God the Son!" said Erinoulla.

"And God the Holy Ghost!" said the rest, in chorus.

Seven black theologians stooped over the spot of wax. The black chorus made the sign of the cross as though they thought the earth would open at their feet. In a few minutes, all the girls of Poli were in Katina's courtyard, dancing in victory.

Katina had seen her future husband, not in a dream, but actually, standing at the window by her bed. Among the maidens of the island, Katina's vision was proclaimed a miracle, and her story became a legend.

Her miracle had an explanation, like all miracles. But if anyone prefers a reason to a miracle—let him draw up his stool and take his place with the black-cowled sophists whose gods have failed. Even they, curiously, did not prefer the reason. Even they kept a cross upon their lips, choosing to celebrate a maid's miracle instead of the dishonor of a maid.

Anezoulla realized it first. She passed on the secret to Erinoulla, who passed it on to Evoudkoulla and on to Marigoulla, Zografoulla, Mangafoulla, and Mertianoulla. From shrouded mouth to shrouded ear, the riddle of the Unknown Deity was undone.

Anezoulla remembered that the alcove off the living room was not Katina's usual sleeping place. She usually slept in the *moussandra* but gave up her place to her sister and her husband for the duration of their visit, and moved to that alcove off the living room where the maid Maria usually slept. So the miracle could be explained.

A man had indeed come and stood in the window by Katina's bed, holding a candle to light his way, and Katina had been awake when she saw him. But this man had not come for Katina, not at all. He had not come for the maid of Poli, but for Maria the maid. And he could have been coming with miraculous regularity, though unlike Katina, Maria had felt no need to boast about it.

In that way, even an Unknown God could be explained. But the seven sisters did not explain him. Instead they adjusted their hoods of office once again, took up their walking sticks, and marched down the road from Poli to Panayia. Within the hour, while there was still a shaving of the sun above Armathia Island, a second defendant was brought before them and a second verdict was secretly pronounced. The maid Maria was turned out forever from their gypsum fortress. That feast of Kleithona, she became the only maid in Kasos who did not rejoice at the discovery of her Unknown God.

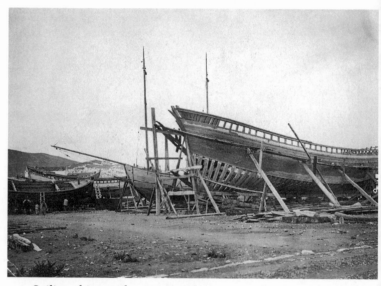

Sailing ships under construction.

LET HIM CAST THE
FIRST STONE

I would be a poor grandson of Kasos if I did not tell something of its shipping history. The land was poor, without water or topsoil, and because a living could not be wrested from it, the islanders turned naturally to the sea.

In 1821, the island put to sea fifteen ships of a hundred tons, mostly brigs and schooners. There were about as many shipping families at that time. The head of the family was captain of the ship, and his younger brothers, cousins, nephews, and the relations of his wife all sailed under his command. That practice endured, to a time when the owners of the ships no longer sail with them. Although Greek shipping has become a multimillion-dollar industry, much of it is still owned and operated in family groups.

During the Egyptian invasion, all the Kasiot ships were captured or destroyed, and the Kasiots had to rebuild their fleet from scratch. Because of the loss they had suffered in 1824, the Kasiots fell behind the wealthier merchants of Hydra and Spetsai, and to regain their position, they had to sail against the wind.

At that time many Kasiots sought a surer livelihood. When the French financier Ferdinand de Lesseps started the Suez Canal, seamen from all over the world migrated to the isthmus to seek employment. A large number of Kasiots were among the first to arrive, and de Lesseps favored them for their seamanship from the beginning.

In the early days of the cutting of the canal, they lived in camps under primitive and unsanitary conditions. Then, after the city of Port Said was founded, they moved into what became a Kasiot quarter. When the Suez Canal was opened in 1869, the first pilot to pass through it was a Kasiot. (Later, when the Panama Canal was opened, its first pilot was also a Kasiot.)

Kasiots became pilots and captains of dredgers, earning salaries many times what they could have earned on sailing ships. Besides their high salaries, they were granted ample pensions and frequent summer vacations. They became the first Greek community in modern Egypt, eventually reaching a population of six thousand.

They learned French and acquired French habits and customs. Through cooperative societies set up by the Canal Company, they bought French goods at reduced prices and preferential duties. By 1890 they had become the envied elite of Kasos, returning to the island during summer months to stroll on their native rock in white suits and shoes and hats from Paris. Uncle George, as a Kasiot boy dressed in the lowly smock of the island children, remembers meeting playmates returned from Egypt in their brilliant white.

Meanwhile, among those who stayed behind, the fifteen brigs and schooners that made up the Kasiot fleet in 1821, had a lively practice of harassing Turkish and Arab merchant vessels. During the Revolution, when the Kasiots blockaded Crete, the neutral governments claimed that because Greece was not a nation and could not legally impose a blockade, these activities of the Kasiots were acts of piracy.

A prodigious scholar of Kasiot history, Dr. Nicholas Mavris, edited *The Archive of Kasos,* a collection of documents referring to the role of Kasos in the Revolution. It contains evidence of constant complaints of the French, British, and Austrian authorities against the Kasiot harassment of neutral ships and attempts to get reparations out of the *Demogerontia* [council of elders] of Kasos.

When the Egyptians finally sacked the island, they found the Kasiot storehouses full of goods obviously stolen from Turkish, Egyptian, or neutral ships. Another source claims that after 1824, when such activities of the Kasiot fleet were at an end, the insurance companies of Trieste and Marseilles actually lowered their rates.

Dr. Mavris has written a pamphlet called "Were the Kasiots Pirates?" in which he attempts to draw a distinction between pirates and corsairs. Pirates, he says, stole for personal gain. Corsairs stole for a political purpose. As Kasiots intercepted only those ships bearing cargoes to the enemy, Dr. Mavris concluded the Kasiots were corsairs.

But if the Kasiots were corsairs, I believe they could also have been pirates. If they could steal for a political purpose, they could also do so for personal gain. Dr. Mavris's own archives contain evidence of Kasiot raids on the neighboring islands of Rhodes and Kos in which they stole provisions not from Turks or Austrians or Englishmen, but from fellow Greeks.

Considering the low opinion the Kasiots had of their landlubbering neighbors the Karpathians, it is safe to assume they stole from them. And we cannot read of the Kasiot exploits during the Revolution without suspecting what they could do before 1821, when such acts could not be interpreted strictly as evidence of piety and patriotism.

Here, the familiar Kasiot saying has another application: "With whatever teacher you sit down with, that's the lesson you will learn." The early Kasiots sat down with Turkish, Venetian, Algerian, and other Arab teachers, and it is inconceivable that they could not only have survived but also flourished under such austere schooling without learning certain lessons all too well. As Kasos itself was within easy striking distance of the trade routes between Constantinople and the outlying provinces of the Ottoman Empire—Crete, Rhodes, Cyprus, Syria, and Egypt—the Kasiots must have had ample opportunity to practice what they learned.

After the Revolution, there was one final eruption of piracy in the Aegean. The French and British fleets worked hard to clean out the islands, and by 1830 piracy was at an end. Now, as Greece took its first steps as a modern nation and began to develop its great potential for a shipping industry, a second dark fact emerges in the history of Kasos.

Even after the end of piracy, there was both an honest and a dishonest way to make a living, for Kasiots as well as other seamen. During the difficult days of the late nineteenth century, an honest captain had to ply the sea continually, accepting any unprofitable cargo for any faraway port (like Captain Elias's roof tiles, which kept him tied up in Syros for a whole winter). Naturally, there were some Kasiot captains who disliked hard work, who preferred to spend their winters on their native island, roistering in the cafés. These Kasiots found another way, the second nefarious maritime practice, known as barratry.

The voyages of sailing ships lasted several weeks. During that time the captain might encounter heavy weather and find himself in danger of sinking unless he lightened his ship by throwing overboard his extra masts, rigging, and even a portion of the cargo. In that event, under the laws of general average, the captain would not be responsible for the loss of cargo, and it would have to be sustained by the cargo owner, who would then recover it from the underwriters.

Here certain captains were cunning enough to see an opportunity. A captain might not encounter heavy weather at all, only *claim* to have encountered it. The coasts of the Aegean Islands and mainland Greece are full of tiny coves, secret places where under the cover of a moonless night a ship might put in unnoticed. A caïque might come out to meet the ship, and the captain might strike a stealthy bargain with the caïque's owner to *sell* him a portion of the cargo.

The captain would direct the crew to unload part of the cargo into the caïque. Then the captain would sail out onto the high seas, and on to the island of

Zante, where there were certain legal consultants who could doctor the log. They would draft their entries *ex post facto* to show that on such and such a day, under the stress of heavy weather, the captain had been forced to jettison his extra masts, spars, and sails (items that might have never existed) and that portion of the cargo he had actually sold.

The captain would thus reap a double profit: the charter hire for transporting the cargo and the proceeds of the sale. Then, his winter's work done in a single voyage, he could return to his native island and roister in the café.

Barratry became widespread after the Revolution; and the Ionian island of Zante, which had been a natural haven for mariners after a storm, became a nest of log doctorers. Gradually, it became so common for captains to put into Zante after selling their cargo that underwriters refused to pay a claim if the ship had stopped there.

Barratry appealed to some Kasiots' wily nature, as much for its own sake as for the profit it would yield. The more brazen ones would sail home to Kasos, anchor outside the Bucca, and sell part of their cargo to the island merchants. Then, sending the ship on to Zante to its doctors, they would ascend victorious to the café.

But no Kasiot ever got rich on barratry. After a captain had sold his cargo, he would be open to blackmail at the hands of his very accomplices; and often in the years ahead, he would have to pay out much more than he had made by the original transaction. Wherever Greek captains were suspected of barratry, the government posted a consul to report any illegal sales, and the Greek government, eager to protect the reputation of its growing merchant marine, ran down offenders and imposed heavy penalties.

Sometime in the latter half of the nineteenth century, a Kasiot captain, whom we can call Captain Markos, put into Salonika to find a cargo. It was a slack season, and for lack of anything better, he contracted to carry a cargo of flagstones at a very unprofitable rate. The cargo belonged to two rabbis, who rubbed salt into his wounds.

"You're a Kasiot, aren't you?" they said.

Captain Markos said he was.

"Well, in that case we shall have to post supercargoes to keep watch over our flagstones."

"Very well," said Captain Markos, taking no offense. "Who will be your supercargoes?"

"We will," said the rabbis. "Both of us."

"You will?" said Captain Markos, smiling. "Very well."

So the rabbis packed their belongings and prepared to sail with Captain Markos to keep watch over their flagstones. In the meantime, the captain was thinking: "Two supercargoes to watch over flagstones? What must they think of me? If I sold all their stones at twice their value, I still would not make enough to pay for my expenses. But let them come if they wish. They will have an exciting voyage."

In the meantime, an idea had grown on him. Captain Markos thought that since the rabbis had heard so much about the mischief of certain Kasiots, he could not very well let them down. As they distrusted him so openly, even with a cargo of flagstones, he would sell their cargo, worthless as it was, under their very noses.

Captain Markos set sail from Salonika, already smirking over what he planned. The two rabbis sailed with him, standing stiffly on either side of the wheel in their black robes and beards and broad-brimmed black hats. They watched Captain Markos with eagle eyes, and when the ship sailed out beyond the harbor, a strong wind came up. Although the rabbis did not realize it, Captain Markos did what any seaman knows not to do. He steered the ship broadside to the wind, so that immediately it began to roll.

"What's that?" asked the rabbis, taken by surprise.

"The wind," said Captain Markos.

"Ah, the wind," said the rabbis solemnly, composing themselves once again. But now the ship was rolling so fiercely they had trouble keeping their balance. They looked at each other without saying a word, and very soon they were both pale as ghosts.

"Is this normal?" said one rabbi at last, in a voice weak with nausea and fear.

"Is the wind normal?" answered Captain Markos.

"What will happen?" said a rabbi, ignoring the captain's invitation to rabbinical disputation.

"I don't know," said Captain Markos, "but you may go below where you can lie down and be more comfortable."

For one longing moment the rabbis looked in the direction of their cabin. Then they looked at each other. But at last, bravely, they decided to stand their ground.

"No, we must stay here to keep watch over our flagstones," they said.

"Very well," said Captain Markos, raising his voice above the wind and water. "But if you must stand here, at least take hold of something. I'm afraid you may be thrown into the sea."

At that moment, appearing to be steering carefully in the face of danger, the captain turned the wheel violently one way and then the other, so that the ship plunged down toward the menacing white water, reprieving itself from catastrophe at the last moment, only to plunge down toward it again on the other side.

"But what is happening?" cried the rabbis. "Is this a storm?"

"Yes," said Captain Markos, "it is a storm."

"Is it a bad one? Is it dangerous?"

"Any storm is a bad one, but this is the most dangerous storm I've ever seen."

"God of Moses. What will happen? Will we drown?"

"We may," said Captain Markos. "We are so heavy and the wind is so strong that at any moment we may go over."

"God of Aaron, is there nothing we can do?"

"Do? What should we do?"

"Is there nothing we can do to save ourselves?"

"Oh, of course there is."

"What?"

"Pray. Pray to your God."

"*Pray to our God?* Is there nothing else?"

"Is that not enough?"

"God of Moses, if we are so heavy, can't we lighten?"

"Lighten? How?"

"If a ship is too heavy, can't we throw some of the cargo overboard?"

"You want me to throw some of the cargo overboard?" said Captain Markos.

"That would save us, wouldn't it?" cried the rabbis. "We would be lighter, and we would be able to make it through this storm."

"That's true. We would be lighter in an instant. The ship would right itself and be out of danger, and there would be an end to this terrible sickness and dizziness and rolling from side to side."

"Oh, dear God of Isaac, let us lighten! God of Jacob, let us throw some of the cargo overboard."

"Upon my honor, as a captain and as a Kasiot, no."

"But why? Why, Captain Markos, in the name of God?"

"Because later, when we reached our destination, you would say we did not meet bad weather at all, and I didn't really throw the cargo overboard but sold it for my own profit. As a Kasiot, I would rather drown than be accused of such a thing."

"Say you sold the cargo? Captain Markos, put it out of your mind! We trust you completely!"

"Then why did you sail with me to watch over your cargo? That is why you find yourselves in this needless danger when you could be safe in your homes this very moment."

By now, the rabbis were close to tears.

"Oh, why, Captain Markos? We do not know! We wish we had never sailed with you. But all that is forgotten. We promise, on the bones of all the prophets, we shall never sail with you again. Only please, captain, throw some of our flagstones overboard. Captain Markos, please, before it is too late."

Captain Markos deliberated for one unendurable moment.

"If you insist," he said. "But one of you must begin. That one." He pointed to one of the rabbis. "Let it be him. Let him cast the first stone."

"I will," said the rabbi. "Only hurry, for the love of God, hurry before all is lost."

Captain Markos directed the crew to open the hatch and lift out one of the stones for the rabbi to throw overboard. Awkwardly, wrestling with the stone on deck until he could maneuver near the side, the rabbi cast the first stone. Afterward, at a signal from Captain Markos, the seamen began to lift out a few more stones and throw them overboard one by one.

Freed of their duties, the rabbis scurried below out of the menacing sea and wind. As soon as they disappeared, Captain Markos ordered his men to stop what they were doing.

"What are you doing there, my lads? Throwing stones into the sea? Have you lost your minds?"

Laughing, the crew stopped throwing stones, closed the hatch, and went about their business. After a discreet interval, Captain Markos steered out of the wind, as any landlubber knows he should. The ship righted itself, and the storm subsided into a placid Aegean afternoon.

The rabbis, by that time, were sound asleep. Delivered from the jaws of death and the terrible nausea, which had menaced them far more, they slept through the dinner hour and into the night. And they were still asleep, near midnight, when Captain

Markos sailed into a deserted cove and, beckoning the owner of a caïque to draw alongside, sold him the remaining flagstones.

The next day, sailing toward their destination on an empty ship, the rabbis signed a paper Captain Markos had prepared, attesting to the fact that the ship had met heavy weather a few miles out of Salonika, and at their insistence, the captain agreed to jettison the cargo. One of the rabbis, they admitted, had cast the first stone.

My father Michael Kulukundis (right), and his brother John aboard their father's ship.

VACATIONS AFLOAT

When the German archaeologist Ludwig Ross visited Kasos in 1847, he saw new ships in the shipyard at Imborio, those of a new Kasiot generation. They were owned by men whose names did not appear on the list of captains in 1821.

My ancestor Elias of the Fez journeyed north to Syros to register his ship *Athena* with the Greek authorities in 1832. His eldest grandson was Captain Elias, and according to Uncle Manuel, Old Elias was still alive in Syros when the young captain was about to take his first command. The old man drew his grandson aside and gave him this advice:

"Son, I want you to know that from the money you earn honestly, the devil will take half. But of the money that comes to you dishonestly, the devil will take all and your soul in the bargain. So my advice to you is to work for your gain and save your money so you may have it when you need it."

Despite the old man's wisdom, Elias of the Fez's eldest son George fared poorly, and about the time of the Crimean War, the family's last ship was lost in a wreck off the island of Scyros (not Syros), leaving the next generation, that of Captain Elias, to start over.

In an inauspicious start, the *Elpis,* the barque that belonged to Captain Elias's brother Nicholas, was lost in 1892, transporting a cargo of marble from Paros to Constantinople. Nicholas's sister was sailing to her wedding with her mother and a beautiful young boy whom her fiancé Nicourezos, the consul in Constantinople, had sent as an envoy to fetch his bride. In addition, the ship was carrying the bride's entire trousseau.

Captain Nicholas was twenty-five, and the *Elpis* was his first command. As he was tacking northward through the Dardanelles, he met another ship, this one commanded by an Albanian captain from the island of Spetsai, going in the same direction on a different tack.

The *Elpis* was a fast ship, and Nicholas wanted to show her off. He passed across the bows of the Albanian although he did not have the right to do so, and the crew of the *Elpis* cheered. On the next tack, he passed before the other ship a second time.

The Albanian shouted, "If you do that again, I'll sink you."

Unable to resist the challenge, Nicholas made a third pass, and this time the Albanian held his course and struck the *Elpis* broadside.

There was hardly enough time to lower a lifeboat. The *Elpis*, loaded with marble, went down like a stone herself. Thrashing in the water, Nicholas seized his sister by the hair and saved her, but before he could do the same for his mother, she drowned. The envoy was drowned as well, and the trousseau lost.

A sailor, an Elias Basil Kulukundis, another grand-son of Elias of the Fez and a cousin of Captain Elias, saved himself by jumping onto the bowsprit of the Albanian ship immediately after impact.

After that, whenever Uncle George and his brothers quarrelled, Captain Elias would scold them by telling this story. He reminded them that he met the Albanian captain once on the waterfront in Syros and didn't provoke him.

"I met the man who drowned my mother," he would say. "I didn't fight, I who had cause, and now you are fighting."

Now the family's fortunes rested with Captain Elias. The captain traded his barque the *Anastasia* from the Black Sea through the Bosporus to Egypt or the western Mediterranean while his wife, Eleni, stayed home with the children. Unless he had a cargo for Alexandria and could stop in Kasos on the way, often he would not return to his native island for eighteen months or a full two years.

That meant that in the summers, when school was over for three months, he would take the boys on board to give his wife a rest and incidentally see something of his sons.

Many of Captain Elias's relations and those of his wife sailed with him as officers and crew, so that the ship became an extended family, whose members teased the children and played with them in the off hours.

Uncle Manuel, Captain Elias's fourth son, wrote a short memoir called "Vacations Afloat" about the transition from sail to steam, which he witnessed at firsthand on board his father's barque and then his steamship. Much of what follows is adapted from his text. I have incorporated the many different voyages of his memoirs and represented them as a single voyage.

The boys, accompanied by Mavrandonis or another relative, set out by ferry from the Bridge of Galata across the Bosporus. As they approached the ferry dock, they saw their father's ship lying at anchor outside the Health Office. When they set foot on deck, carrying all the belongings they would need for the summer, Captain Elias ordered the crew to weigh anchor, and the ship set off for Braila, in Rumania, to load grain for Marseilles.

It was hot in this port at the mouth of the Danube, and they were accustomed to eating on deck, burning small patties of manure in lanterns to keep off mosquitoes.

Captain Elias completed loading with a shipment of lumber for Messina in Sicily, which had been destroyed by an earthquake. As they prepared to weigh anchor, a boatman with watermelons came alongside. The watermelons of Braila were exceptionally sweet, so Captain Elias ordered the crew to buy the boatman's entire supply. Many of the watermelons were loaded into the lifeboats, and those for the captain's table were put in the captain's bathtub. (I would have done the same in the captain's place. Why take a bath when you can be assured of a constant supply of watermelon?)

A whole beef carcass was also brought on board. In those days before refrigeration, the crew was detailed to salt the beef, and the boys, the younger ones dressed in short pants and sailor caps, assisted in the process. The sailors made shallow cuts in the meat, which the boys then laced with salt. The salted pieces were put dry into special barrels, so that a few days later, when the sea had washed over the barrels, the meat would be swimming in brine.

Captain Elias acted as a mentor to his relatives and a valued adviser to other owners. But in my view, he was not what would be called "a nurturing father." He had a sharp tongue, which he could wield like a whip. Once, having tasted the soup that the cook had just placed before him, he handed the bowl back and told the cook to take out some of the salt.

"How can I do that, Captain?" said the bewildered cook.

"If you can't take it out, why do you put it in?" said the captain, giving the cook a slap.

The boys, as well as the crew, lived in awe of this figure at the head of the table, who commanded their lives at sea and required total silence when he sat at his desk.

Once George got in trouble for losing half of the ship's meat supply. He was in charge of watching the two billy goats kept on deck. As the ship passed the Aegean island of Anti-Melos, one of the goats smelled some comrades exiled on the island and, wishing to join them, jumped overboard.

Another time Nicholas, trying to make himself useful, supervised the intake of drinking water but let his attention wander at the crucial moment and failed to see that the tank was full, so that the water overflowed, flooding the tweendeck and damaging part of the grain cargo.

My father's brothers Uncle John (left) and Uncle George on board an R & K ship in the 1930s.

"Avaria del mare," the captain wrote ambiguously in his log (damage at sea), thus protecting his son.

The two older boys regularly incurred their father's displeasure. Only Manuel seemed always to stay on the captain's good side. He thrived on his father's favor and became his protégé.

Manuel went on to become a dominant figure in the history of Greek shipping in the twentieth century, and I include a small portrait of him here.

Uncle Manuel was tall. (He liked to say he was the tallest Kulukundis until I came along.) With a tall man's stature and a chubby man's disposition, he was the most successful of the brothers, and he founded the venerable London ship-broking firm of Rethymnis and Kulukundis with his father, Captain Elias, in the 1920s.

Uncle Manuel had a round face and curly black hair, and he wore thick round glasses. He had a jolly laugh, was very good-natured and at ease, and he liked to be in the thick of whatever was going on. When we were children, we called him "Uncle Monopoly," which amused him mightily.

In later years, after I got over reacting to feeling patronized by his sometimes didactic manner, I could appreciate Uncle Manuel's talents more fully. When my daughter Delia was a toddler, trying to handle everything she could reach in my parents' house, instead of shouting at her and pinioning her arms to her sides as everybody else wanted to do, Uncle Manuel drew her to him and engaged her interest by tapping his cane on the black and white squares of our cocktail porch floor. In this way, he kept her attention for at least half an hour.

Uncle Manuel with son Michael and nephews Dimitri and Tony Manthos at the Westchester Country Club.

In the same way, he seemed genuinely interested in encouraging young people. Like most Greek men of his generation, certainly those in my family, he was not much for asking you questions or listening to your views; but at least he made an effort to explain what was going on.

Manuel had been close to his father, and from his youth, he'd had the Captain's ear.

"*Faflatas*," Uncle Nicholas, the second brother, called him (Sweet-talker). Less self-assured than Manuel, Nicholas was nonetheless not retiring like Uncle George and compensated for his lack of confidence with bluster and bravado. (All the brothers except Uncle George, truth be told, had a tendency toward pontification. Even as mild a man as my uncle John, the fourth brother, widely loved and repeatedly elected president of the London Ship Owners' Association, could express some quite firm views.

As the eldest brother, George should have been the one to assume the leadership of the family business, but he was unsuited to the role, by both temperament and inclination. From an early age he was awkward with his father and naïve in his dealings with him. When he was about to graduate from the American College of Beirut, he wrote Captain Elias to say that he wished to take the faith of his educators and become a Protestant. The captain was outraged. A family scandal ensued, and the younger but more reliable Manuel was dispatched to bring George, the eldest, to his senses.

From a young age, Uncle Manuel had poor eyesight, and used to watch enviously as his playmate and future partner Minas Rethymnis would dive forty feet from the deck of the steamship *Chrysopolis,* owned by the Rethymnis-Yannaghas-Pneumaticos partnership (my godfather, maternal grandfather, and great-uncle) to the water below.

Manuel was not capable of any such feats of athletic prowess. Nor did he strive for recognition in other ways. While his older brothers Nicholas and George busied themselves with useful tasks on board their father's ship, Manuel was content to be a passenger and occupied himself with his father's binoculars, taking pride in being able to identify any vessel he saw on the horizon of the Mediterranean or the Black Sea. Later he used this prodigious visual knowledge of maritime history, together with considerable skill as a watercolorist, to re-create maritime scenes from memory.

Manuel had an innate sense of belonging wherever he was, with no need to make himself useful. He did not need to seek favor because he already had favor. Why one son has that and another does not is a matter I cannot explain, but it was clear that Manuel had his father's favor from the beginning and never lost it.

In his memoirs, Manuel wrote candidly about what he called his lazy nature, but in my view, it was the kind of laziness that is useful to cultivate.

The image of him standing on the bridge of his father's ship, scanning the horizon with binoculars, while his more industrious elder brothers scurried to make themselves useful, personifies to me the essence of the entrepreneur. More than anyone in the family Manuel had the leisure of mind to look beyond the details of the working day to see what lay ahead. That attitude did not always sit well with his brothers, especially since he often let them know that he considered them to be the passengers. Nevertheless, as I was starting out in business, I had no doubt which model—Manuel or his brothers—was the one to emulate.

At Uncle John's funeral in 1980, I had a glimpse of Uncle Manuel's instinct for self-promotion. In Saint Sophia Cathedral in London, the three surviving brothers—Uncle Manuel, Uncle Nicholas, and my father—stood in the front row of mourners. When it was time for people to pass in front of the bier and shake hands with the bereaved, Manuel found himself wedged awkwardly between Nicholas and my father. Instead of continuing to feel uncomfortable in that position, he simply stepped out of the row, turned adroitly and faced at right angles to his brothers. Now he was standing in the aisle, so that people had to greet Nicholas and my father first, as a kind of warm-up to the main event, then turn the corner and pay their respects to him.

He was, as my wife Lucy said, "not backward in coming forward." But he handled self-advancement with charm, grace, and a certain amount of humor, which, among the elders who dominated my growing up, made him another oasis in a desert, a different kind of oasis from Uncle George.

After unloading lumber in Messina, the boys saw the rail ferries passing between the tip of Sicily and Reggio di Calabria on the Italian boot.

In those days, before the advent of radio, Lloyd's maintained signal stations at strategic points to report ships' movements. At the straits between the two promontories that personified the legendary monsters Scylla and Charybdis in the *Odyssey,* Captain Elias gave the order to hoist a set of four international flags so that the ship's passage would be reported in *Lloyd's List*, then as now the newspaper of record of the shipping industry.

Setting out northward toward Naples, they passed the volcano Mt. Stromboli, and the captain handed his binoculars to Manuel so that he could see the flames and the red-hot lava spewing from the crater. Manuel handed them on to George and Nicholas, and Captain Elias informed his sons that Europe's three active volcanoes, Aetna, Stromboli, and Vesuvio, were all within a hundred miles of each other.

In the evening they approached the Bay of Naples, and to their surprise they heard anguished cries coming from the water. The officer of the watch stopped the ship and Captain Elias ordered a dinghy to be let down. They discovered several people—a mother, two sons, and three daughters, in addition to a boatman—clinging desperately to the hull of a sailboat.

A Neapolitan family named Poppi had hired the boat to take a trip up the bay to see a battleship the Italian government had put on exhibit. On their return, just as they were entering the Bay of Naples, the wind came up and a sudden gust capsized them. They had been in the water for hours, and later they said they could not have held on much longer.

The Italian Ministry of Merchant Marine sent Captain Elias a bronze medal with an accompanying diploma that read: "Il Ministro della Marina a concesso una medaglia commemoratia di bronzo al Capitano Elias Kulukundis."

In the meantime, the family expressed their gratitude by bringing gifts, cash gratuities to the crew, and toys for Captain Elias's children. Uncle George told me these were the first toys the children had ever had. Captain Elias would bring them clothes from the far-off ports he visited, but evidently he did not see the purpose of toys.

Proceeding northward, they passed the Straits of Bonifacio, dotted with little islets and marked with buoys and lighthouses. But they did not enter them. This passage between Corsica and Sardinia is a direct route from Sicily to Marseilles, but the mistral was blowing from France, and the captain sailed north to Genoa.

Before they entered the gulf, they saw Elba, where

Napoleon was first exiled, and the island of Monte
Cristo, where Alexander Dumas's hero found the
treasure in *The Count of Monte Cristo*.

Once alongside the quay in Genoa, Captain Elias
left the ship in the hands of the first mate and went
up to town. By suppertime the boys were delighted to
see him appear in the distance, returning with a white
parcel, which meant he had been to the *pasticceria*.

Everybody likes to trace a spiritual inheritance
from his ancestors. Another way I feel connected to
my grandfather (besides our common interest in
watermelon) is by our love of opera. In those days,
every little Italian port had a company, and whenever
Captain Elias moored his ship, he would hand over
command to the first mate and go off to the matinee.

He knew all the Italian repertory and had seen
some operas dozens of times. He passed on his passion to his sons, particularly Uncle Manuel and my
father, who for many years had subscriptions at the
Metropolitan Opera in New York.

During my Christmas vacation from Exeter in
1954, my father gave me two tickets to *Faust* he could
not use. I invited a girl I had just met and wanted to
impress. And at the age of sixteen, I in a dinner jacket
and she in a black velvet cape, we toddled off to the
Old Met on Fortieth Street (a different sort of vacation from those in "Vacations Afloat").

But my father didn't tell me that Uncle Manuel
had a subscription on the same night, and before the
lights went down for the overture, I had the feeling
of eyes upon me and looked over my shoulder to see
Uncle Manuel and Aunt Calliope upstairs in their

box. This time the family binoculars were in the hands of my aunt as she gave my date and me the once-over from top to bottom.

In the first act, when Faust sang "Come to me Satan," as though at his command, a suave man with a silken voice ascended on a circular platform through the floor, and I first heard Cesare Siepi. When I was a teenager, I used to get myself going in the morning by listening to Beethoven as soon as I woke up. Now I put on a CD of Siepi.

Captain Elias was one of the first of his contemporaries to foresee that the era of sail was coming to an end, and in 1898 he decided to sell the *Anastasia*. His prospects were precarious, as the price he could get for her was just enough to buy a minority interest in a steamship. But like many people who are skilled at making decisions, he knew that doing nothing would be riskier than taking a step.

So he presented himself to some wealthy merchants of Syros, including the owner of a tanning factory, Alexios Gangos. He offered to contribute his know-how and all his life savings, and he proposed that if the merchants would put in the rest of the capital, they should buy a steamship together. He found a suitable ship; the merchants were willing; and the new partnership bought the *Leni*, which renamed the *Alexios Gangos* in honor of the principal shareholder. Captain Elias, as an eleven percent shareholder, took command.

About eighty years later, after I had entered the shipping business, I approached a New York investment bank to support my purchase of two tankers at prices then at a historic low. The bank asked how much money I would be putting in, and I said eleven percent and mentioned that it was exactly the size of my grandfather's stake in his first steamship.

I admit, as the venture came closer to reality, I reduced my share to ten per cent, as eleven would have included the value of our piano and silverware, which my wife, Lucy, was loath to let be part of the deal. Even then, there was a precedent, as my grandmother Eleni's jewelry was pledged to the bank as collateral for the loan that purchased the *Leni*.

The *Alexios Gangos* was wrecked in the winter of 1905 off the coast of Sicily, and in 1906 the same partnership bought the *Proteus* to replace her. The venture flourished and soon the partners were able to purchase another vessel, the *Katina*, named for Gangos's wife.

Here some trouble began. Mrs. Katina Gangos, though older than my grandfather, took an immediate liking to him. She had the habit of traveling with the ship without her husband and made no attempt to hide her attraction for the young captain. Members of the crew used to tease Uncle George and his brothers, saying, "Your father will divorce your mother and marry Mrs. Gangos."

While the *Katina* was waiting for a berth to discharge grain in Marseilles, which sometimes could take weeks, Mrs. Gangos asked the captain to accompany her to Paris. Captain Elias's nickname was "the Bishop" and sometimes "the Saint," and the crew usually stood at attention when they saw him coming. Here "the Saint" found himself in difficulty for he would be damned if he did and damned if he didn't, as

Captain Elias, nicknamed The Saint.

the lady could give her husband a poor report of him either way.

But if Captain Elias was a saint, at least he was a clever one, and at the decisive moment, he hit on a smooth move. He said he could not leave the ship, but appointed his first mate (and first cousin) Elias Martis Kulukundis to accompany the lady to Paris in his stead, "since Elias Martis knew French," was my Uncle Manuel's comment. Uncle Manuel liked to say things diplomatically, but as usual, Uncle George told you what was really going on. The strategem kept the lady happy, and in the captain's debt, and Captain Elias retained both sainthood and his job.

The author and Uncle George in Kasos. (Photo by Robert McCabe)

THE HOLLOW CROWN

Sometime before the end of the nineteenth century, an eligible doctor named Dimitri Nikolakis tried to solve the riddle of how a man should marry. Kasiot marriages were arranged by the families of the bride and groom in what was known as *proxenia*.

In this process, the initiative must come from the woman's family. A man could not simply ask a girl to marry him, or people would think he was so ineligible he could not get a wife any other way. At a feast on the square before the church, as he looked the girl's father carefully in the eye, he might sing a *mandinadha:*

"A flower blooms in your courtyard,
Fairer than all others on the island."

Everyone would think it a forced and empty rhyme, but to the girl's father the rhyme would not be empty at all. If he found the bridegroom to his liking, he and his male relations would wait for the next moonless evening to put on socks of different colors and, holding a lantern before them to light their way, they would pay the man a visit.

If their *proxenia* was accepted, the party would come home singing *mandinadhas,* and by morning everyone would know of the impending marriage. But if the answer was equivocal in the least, the delegates would come home as silently as they had gone out, with even the lantern burning furtively.

Dimitri had a brother, Yani, and a sister, Eloula. Their father had been lost at sea when the children were very young. Their mother was a strong-willed Kasiot woman, who had worn black most of her life and brought up her children alone. She had doted on her firstborn, Dimitri, who had always been first in his class and went to study medicine in Athens.

Beside this prince, Yani, the second son, was practically forgotten. He used to spend his afternoons in the fields and vineyards, stealing fruit from under the eyes of the watchmen hiding in the trees. And it was not long before he roamed the fields in the evening, after a different kind of fruit, with Karpathian working girls, far from home and parents, willing to spend the night on the floors of unfinished houses, kicking at the moon.

"When are you getting married, Yani?" said one of the old men in the café, and the suggestion would be greeted by great laughter, for no one thought Yani Nikolakis likely to receive a delegation on a moonless night.

But the joke was on the old men of the Bucca after all, and on the Kasiot marriage system. For at that moment, Yani's wedding bed was prepared—in an abandoned sheepfold in the hills—and he had already chosen the girl to take to it: Calliope, the fourth daughter of Captain Vassilis, a not-too-wealthy gentleman from Panayia.

Yani thought her beautiful, though others might say she was too short. And though some said she was feebleminded, giggling foolishly the way she did, Yani thought her cheerful and good-natured. In short, he loved her, and he was blind to her faults, including the outstanding one that as a fourth daughter, she obviously would have no dowry.

One day Yani saw Calliope buying fruit in Phry.

"Sleep in your *moussandra* tonight," he said, standing next to her, turning a melon in his hands.

In Calliope's house, the *moussandra* opened onto a balcony that extended out beyond the courtyard wall. It was too high for people walking in the street to reach it, but a man riding by on muleback, taking hold of the railing, could swing himself up.

"And leave the window open."

Calliope did as she was told, for a reason not hard to understand. For if a fourth daughter of a not-too-wealthy captain is so timorous that she lets such a chance go by, she deserves the life of spinsterhood bound to follow.

After midnight, Yani rode his mule downhill, past the cemetery, through the narrow labyrinthine streets of Phry, and uphill toward the village of Panayia.

In the meantime, in the *moussandra*, Calliope lay in the dark, fully clothed, her black eyes shining above her blankets. Suddenly, in the silence, the shutters parted and a man's figure appeared on the balcony, framed against the sky.

"Come," he whispered.

And Calliope came.

Yani wrapped the blanket around her and jumped onto the mule ahead of her. Following him, completely trusting, Calliope fell into his arms.

Yani's heart was beating wildly as they rode away, two of them in one saddle, the mule's footsteps falling in the streets of Panayia as gently as summer hail. Outside Panayia, Yani turned the mule across the plain toward Arvanitohori. He had no more thought for silence now, shouting to the mule and striking its haunches with his stick.

Now they were alone on that deserted plain, barren and sharply rutted with volcanic rock. They made their way across the bed of a rain torrent, riding uphill toward Arvanitohori. Then, just below the town, Yani slipped down and led the mule across the rocky bed, Calliope holding fast to the saddle, still wrapped in her blanket: a virgin fleeing to the promised land.

Across the torrent Yani mounted again, and prodded the mule up to a road high on the shoulders of the mountain, across a huge canyon opening like a lesion in the rock. They rode carefully along the canyon's rim, past the chapel of the Prophet Elias high on the mountain, until they found the sheepfold, sheltered beneath a cliff.

There, in that homely bower, they had a ceremony stripped of all custom but the essential one, which any bridegroom knows and any bride can learn. Later in the week, Captain Vassilis would give his daughter to Yani Nikolakis (what could he do?) but that evening, without his assistance, in the hills near Arvanitohori, Calliope married him herself.

The next day, when the "wedding" was announced, it became the event of that bridal season. The captain was wise enough to remember that this unexpected marriage had cost him nothing. Kasiot custom had no authority over such a revolutionary marriage, but it granted no advantage either. Once a man had stolen his bride, he could not then stop to negotiate a dowry without bringing the bullets of her kinsmen raining on his head.

For her part, Mother Nikolakis cared just as much for this latest adventure of her second son as she did for his earlier ones.

"Let Yani do whatever he wants," she said. "My son the doctor will make the brilliant match."

In the meantime, for Dimitri, lately returned from medical school in Athens, she sang golden prophecies.

"The girl you marry will be clever and obedient, respectful and intelligent," she said. "She must have not only a house and dowry, but also fields and vineyards falling to her name in all the regions of the island. She must have mills and sheepfolds, chapels and holy icons and many gold napoleons woven on her breast with golden thread. She must be the first daughter of a first daughter, descended in direct lineage from a noble Kasiot family, a true princess of the island."

"Who is she?" said Dr. Nikolakis. "Who is the noble daughter you have in mind?"

"I don't know," his mother said. "I don't even know where to find her. You have the right to expect such perfection in a woman. I'm afraid there is not one girl in Kasos worthy to become your bride."

Dimitri Nikolakis was indeed an eligible man.

He was tall and slender, with a well-trimmed black mustache and two curls separating gracefully in the middle of his forehead. His hair was combed, and he wore a frock coat and a high stiff collar with a firmly tied bow tie.

When he first arrived on Kasos, the island was stricken with an epidemic. Never had the Kasiot sun beat down more terribly, never had the "eye" worked greater evil. He had not been on Kasos more than a few days when nearly every family in Ayia Marina suffered a case of sunstroke or some other ill. The epidemic spread to Phry and Arvanitohori, then to Poli and Panayia. Even the island's midwife and exorcist could find no charms against the blight.

The only charm belonged to Dr. Nikolakis. Adjusting his tie and teasing his curls before every excursion, he visited every house, where, miraculously, on his arrival the patient would sit up in bed (invariably it was a young, unmarried girl) and her astonished mother would make a dozen crosses and swear that only an hour before the girl had trouble to open her eyes. Then, forgetting the miracle as instantly as it had occurred, the mother would lead the doctor off into the *salla,* inquire politely after his mother, and ply him with cognac and a sweet of the spoon.

Dimitri Nikolakis was fond of spending the afternoons with Captain Markos Phillipides and his brothers at their house in Panayia. One day Captain Markos said, "Well, Dr. Nikolakis, your younger brother is already married; it won't be long before you take the crown." The next day he said, "Doctor, your younger brother married a girl from Panayia. Surely our town can do as well for you."

Teasing his curls and adjusting his tie, Dr. Nikolakis lowered his eyes and pretended he had not understood the hint. But he *had* understood. And he was thinking of the prospect more and more. As he did so, he came more often than ever to Captain Phillipides' courtyard.

The family took these visits as a counter-hint, an indication that Dr. Nikolakis would accept a proposal if it were offered. One afternoon, all the Phillipides males were sitting in the courtyard: Captain Markos, his younger brother Stavros, and his elder brother Petros, who was a little deaf. The town was quiet except for the occasional clatter of donkeys' footsteps in the streets.

"By the way, Doctor," Captain Markos said at last, bravely beating back the silence, "you know my daughter?"

Captain Markos's daughter, Fifika, was known throughout the island as clever and obedient, respectful and intelligent. She had fields and vineyards, and many napoleons woven on her breast with golden thread. She was a first daughter of a first daughter.

"I mean Fifika, my first daughter," continued Captain Markos in a low voice.

"Of course," muttered Dimitri, "Fifika, your first daughter."

"You've seen her in church on Sundays and at the village feasts."

"Oh yes," said the doctor, "in church on Sundays and at the village feasts."

"Of course," said Captain Markos mournfully, and in another moment they lapsed into silence again.

"She's a fine girl," said Dr. Nikolakis, to give the captain some encouragement.

"Then you appreciate my daughter's virtues?"

"Oh, I do," said Dimitri eagerly.

Captain Markos felt better and moved his stool closer to the doctor's. "She has a house and everything inside it, crockery and silverware for a queen's table and linen for a queen's bed. She has fields and vineyards, mills and sheepfolds, chapels and holy icons. Now what do you say to that?"

"Wh-what should I say, Captain Markos?" said Dr. Nikolakis. "If she had nothing else, Fifika would be lucky to be born your daughter."

"What's that?" asked brother Petros, a hand cupped around his ear.

"He says *she is a fine girl,*" said Captain Markos.

"We *know* that," said brother Petros. "We've been sitting here all afternoon, and all he can say is what we know already."

"All in good time," said Captain Markos, winking at the doctor. "Doctor, when you have seen my daughter at the village feasts, have you noticed she has many sovereigns and napoleons threaded on her breast?"

"Indeed!" whispered Dimitri.

"You've noticed."

"Indeed I have," said the doctor. Then, believing he may have been indiscreet, he added, "But I do not value the gold that adorns the person so much as the person who adorns the gold."

"What a tongue this fellow has in his head!" said Captain Markos, slapping the doctor on the knee. "He has such command of Romaic, you hardly know what he's saying."

"What *is* he saying?" asked deaf brother Petros.

"He says he likes her," said brother Stavros.

"Then if he *likes* her, will he *marry* her?"

"That, no doubt," said Captain Markos, "is the very next thing we shall learn from him. We all agree that Fifika is a fine girl, and the doctor has just told us with his usual eloquence that, in plain language, he likes her. Now all we need to know is whether he will have her for his wife."

Dr. Nikolakis stammered.

"O-only a madman would decline to have her," he said. "No man in his senses would decline to make his life among you with fair Fifika for his wife."

"What does he say?" said brother Petros, a hand upon his ear.

"He says *yes!*" said brother Stavros.

"I thought he'd keep us here all night," said Petros.

"*Bravo,* Dr. Nikolakis," said Captain Markos.

"Welcome to our family," said brother Stavros.

"Glory to God," said brother Petros. "And now, if you'll excuse me, I'm going to bed. With all this talk I'm perfectly exhausted."

On the way home, Dimitri Nikolakis realized to his surprise that his hands were trembling and his heart was beating wildly. Why should that be, for there was really nothing remarkable in what had happened. At last, the proposal had come, and he had accepted it as he knew he would. He had just become engaged to Fifika Phillipides and was going to tell his mother.

He didn't know why he was running, but he was

running just the same. He ran up the road beyond the Bucca, past the contorted jungles of prickly pears, past carob and olive trees with shadows dancing in the setting sun. He reached the town of Ayia Marina and ran through the narrow pebbled streets, among the houses huddled together like ascending stairs.

The bell was tolling at the church, the gates to courtyards swung ajar, and in the doorways stood hooded women—mothers, aunts, grandmothers—calling urchins from their play. In the rising wind of evening, the town was summoning its offspring with a woman's voice. And Dr. Nikolakis heard the call and hurried to his mother.

He opened the gate, as uneasy and cautious as any other child come home from mischief that afternoon. When his mother saw him, she cried, "Bring sugared almonds to welcome him and sacks of speckled pepper!" And she kissed him on either cheek.

The three hooded Nikolakis women who lived with his mother said:

"May the Virgin bless your arrival."

"May your house be full of heirs."

"May your name never vanish from the island."

By that time, Dr. Nikolakis had some definite suspicions. Did the intention to marry show on a man's face? Were women so attentive to this matter they could sense a wedding before it was announced?

"She's a fine girl," his mother said. "Clever and obedient, respectful and intelligent. She has fields and vineyards, chapels and holy icons, and many gold napoleons woven on her breast. She is not all that you deserve, but to do her justice, no one has claimed she *does* deserve you. They have simply offered you her hand and a large dowry to go with it. So, in that case, I think she will do very nicely."

"I'm glad you like her," muttered Dr. Nikolakis, but secretly he was thinking: How could she know? Could the news of a man's *proxenia* travel faster than his feet?

"Glad I *like* her?" his mother said. "Of course I like her."

"Then you aren't angry I didn't tell you about it first?"

"Didn't tell me about it first? How could you? It only just happened."

"That's what I was thinking. But how did you know? I've just come from there."

"What do you mean, come from where?" said Mother Nikolakis.

"From the Phillipides. I spent the whole afternoon with them."

"And what of that? You are always wasting your time with them," said Mother Nikolakis. "Who's talking about the Phillipides?"

"Who are you talking about?"

"The Yeroyioryis."

"The Yeroyioryis?"

"And their first daughter, Marika."

"Their first daughter Marika?"

"Only an hour ago, Captain Manoli Yeroyioryis and his two brothers were right here where we are standing, making the proposal."

"They were? And what did you say?"

"I said *yes*. They knew I would, as it was only my little hint that gave them nerve to make the proposal in the first place."

"And what did *they* say?"

"They were very happy. Oh, they said, just as a formality, they would like to talk to you themselves. They'll be back tomorrow morning, so do talk to them please, as a favor to me. You are over thirty now, and your poor mother wouldn't dream of influencing you. So tomorrow, when they come, tell them it's settled. Next Sunday, we'll hold the engagement ceremony and the *prikosimfonon* will be signed. And two Sundays from now you'll be married. Oh, dear boy, I can hardly believe this has happened."

"I can hardly believe it either," said Dimitri.

That night, for many sleepless hours, Dr. Nikolakis pondered his first turning on the road to marriage.

He knew very well what the Yeroyioryis' would come to hear, and he knew his task in the morning would be to avoid that proposal he could not accept, without actually refusing it, as that too would be impossible, owing to the fact that his mother had already accepted it on his behalf.

If he had chosen revolution then, he could have solved his problem. He could have ignored the custom, as his younger brother had, and told the Yeroyioryis family he would marry Fifika Phillipides, the girl he wanted. But the doctor was not a revolutionary, not yet in any case.

"Only a madman would decline to have her," he said to Captain Yeroyioryis and his two brothers. "No man in his senses would decline to make his life among you with fair Marika for his wife."

"Then it's settled," said Captain Manoli

Yeroyioryis, getting up to kiss Dr. Nikolakis on both cheeks.

Dimitri raised his arms to stop him. "If only it were settled," he said, "I would be the happiest man in Kasos."

"It isn't settled?" said the captain.

"No," said the doctor, "and for the time being, I'm afraid it cannot be. You see, gentlemen, I have a sister. Eloula is her name, and she has reached the age of twenty, when she herself is ready to be married. And you know, gentlemen, if a girl's male relations do not help her find a husband, how will she find a husband on her own? You understand that, or you yourselves would not have come here this morning. A custom of our island brings your generous offer to me, and the very same custom prevents me from accepting it. You come to me to fulfill a gentle duty, and as that duty is fulfilled, so, at the same time, must it remain unfulfilled. Only by remaining unfulfilled can that gentle duty find fulfillment."

"What does he say?" asked one of the Yeroyioryis brothers.

"I'm not sure," said Captain Manoli. "He says he can't marry her for the time being."

"Why not?"

"Because he has a sister."

After the Yeroyioryis brothers had gone, Mrs. Nikolakis rushed in like a virago after vengeance.

"Are you in your senses?" she asked. "What made you say such things?"

"My duty," said Dr. Nikolakis.

"Squashes and cucumbers for your duty! Is this

my reward, to be repaid with your disobedience and disrespect?"

"On the contrary," said Dimitri. "I am observing the custom of the island, and in doing so, I am most obedient and respectful."

"Squashes and cucumbers for the custom. What help does Eloula need from you to find a husband? What help could you be to her, as you could not even find yourself a wife? When the time comes, I will find her a husband, just as I've found a wife for you. But she is too young to marry yet. For the time being, I want her with me."

"Then you shall have her," said Dimitri, "and for the time being, you shall have me too."

"Christ and Virgin!" said Mother Nikolakis. "I don't know which of my sons is the greater curse, the one who never listens to a word I say or the one who is so obedient."

Dimitri Nikolakis had another errand to do that morning. He changed his collar, combed his hair, and then set out for Panayia.

The Phillipides were glad to see him, for they had heard disquieting news the night before. But his appearance did not comfort them. He burst into their courtyard, delivered them the very same oration on the subject of his duty that he had just delivered to the Yeroyioryis family, and, a moment later, departed as suddenly as he had come.

"What did he say?" said brother Petros.

"He said he cannot marry Fifika for the time being," said Captain Markos.

"He can't?"

"Not until his sister finds a husband."

"But why didn't he think of that before? You don't think the Yeroyioryis have a hand in this? You don't believe what they were saying that the doctor's *proxenia* was announced in Ayia Marina yesterday, to Marika Yeroyioryis?"

"How could that be," said Captain Markos, "when it was concluded to our own Fifika? You were right here when I concluded it."

"I thought so."

"He sat right there and told us only a madman would decline to have Fifika."

"So let us hope he is not a madman."

"He said no man in his senses would decline to make his life among us with fair Fifika for his wife."

"So let's hope he's in his senses," said brother Petros. "Unfortunately, that was not the impression I had of him this morning."

"Nonsense, brother. Concern for an unmarried sister is evidence of a faithful nature. And a faithful nature is a virtue, brother, even in a husband."

"I have nothing against virtue in a husband," said Petros, "as long as he's a husband. Let Dr. Nikolakis marry our Fifika first, then he can be as faithful as he wants."

But all the Phillipides' could do, in their courtyard in Panayia, was to wait and see, which was precisely what the Yeroyioryis' could do, in their courtyard in Ayia Marina. The next Sunday was the first of three carnivals. People went around the streets in masks and antic costumes, eating and drinking far into the night. The Monday after the last Carnival Sunday would be Pure Monday, and the day after that was the beginning of Lent, and after that, no one could be married for forty days until Easter.

"What are you going to do?" the doctor's sister Eloula asked him when he came home.

"Nothing," said Dimitri, collapsing in an armchair, "I'll buy time. In two weeks, the carnivals will be over. Once Lent has started, no one can be married for forty days. If I can make it to the Tuesday after the last Monday, I'll be free."

"But you're not trying to be free, Dimitri. You're trying to get married."

"I know. But to which one?"

"The one you want?"

"Fifika?"

"Marry her quickly, Dimitri. Steal her, like Yani. Her family will help you. If you let love slip away from you, it may never come back."

For Eloula, the course was easy. She believed in love and had often said that she would not marry until she found it.

That evening there was no moon. Two black-cowled old ladies, Sofitsa and Kalitsa, were sitting on a threshold in Ayia Marina when three figures passed by their gate, holding a lantern to guide their way.

"Proxenia!" said Sofitsa.

"I wonder who," said Kalitsa.

On silent slippers, Sofitsa and Kalitsa went out into the street, and there they saw Captain Manoli Yero-yioryis and his two brothers. They stopped at the house of another old seafarer of Ayia Marina, Captain Manoussos, whose first son, Andoni, was still a bachelor.

"They've given up the doctor," Sofitsa whispered. "You don't need theology to know that. Now, to save face, they are hurrying to conclude their daughter's *proxenia* to Andoni Manoussos."

But Sofitsa was wrong and not even theology would have helped her know the answer. The Yeroyioryis had not given up the doctor, not at all. It was true their moonless mission was a *proxenia,* but not on behalf of their daughter Marika. They had come to ask for Andoni Manoussos's hand in marriage for a young Kasiot girl who was in no way their relation. Not yet, in any case. They were performing this *proxenia* on the authority of the doctor's mother, and the girl whose hand they offered was the doctor's sister, Eloula.

Though Eloula had been too young for marriage in the morning, by evening her time had come. A virtuous girl attending to her mother, she became the helpmate to her lord and master, and went through that transformation in a single day.

"Dimitri, help me," said Eloula, running in to see the doctor when she heard the news. "Why have you done this?"

In spite of himself, Dimitri was shocked. "Eloula, I haven't done it. I knew nothing about it. I'm as much victim of what's happening as you are."

"But it's *your* fate," Eloula said, "not mine. What do I owe for it?"

And to that, the doctor had no answer.

According to the custom, the next ceremony in the marriage process would be the *emvasmata,* or formal betrothal, when the bridegroom would step across the girl's threshold for the first time as her bridegroom-to-be. Before the man could take this irrevocable step, the girl's father had to sign a document called the *prikosimfonon,* in which he would list the items of his daughter's dowry, her house and lands, and the sum of cash he had provided for her.

On Sunday, the combined families gathered at the Manoussos house for the signing of the *prikosimfonon.* After Andoni's had been signed, Dr. Nikolakis rose to recite his sister's. (What could he do? He had appealed to custom, and now he must follow wherever it should lead.)

"In this fair and benevolent hour that has come upon us," he began, in the traditional form of the Kasiot *prikosimfonon,* "I, Dimitri Nikolakis, hereby establish familial relations between myself and Captain Yani Manoussos of Ayia Marina and accept his first son Andoni as a bridegroom for my pure and virgin sister Eloula."

As he said that, Dr. Nikolakis tried not to look at his sister, who was just then standing as a prisoner between her mother and Captain Manoussos.

"First I give her my blessing and the blessing of our mother and of all our family, and then I give her all the following: the house she lives in and all its contents, including six blankets, twelve bedsheets, four pillows . . ."

It was a laborious recitation. No one was interested in pillows and bedsheets. What everyone was waiting to hear was the sum of hard cash that would accompany Eloula's hand.

Dr. Nikolakis went on, about a vineyard near the cemetery and a grazing plot near the rain-torrent. At last, undoing a wine-red handkerchief, he let its contents fall on the table before the notary.

"In addition," he said, "I give her fifty golden sovereigns."

It was a modest sum, and it produced a modest murmur. But it was almost the total cash resources of the Nikolakis family. Dr. Nikolakis surrendered it freely, for in a very short time, if he married either Fifika Phillipides or Marika Yeroyioryis, he would receive many times the total in return.

"Fifty golden sovereigns," said the notary, after counting out the coins. "Is it agreed?"

"Agreed!" said Andoni Manoussos.

"Agreed!" said Andoni's mother and father.

"Agreed!" said all the influential elders of the island.

From the rear of the *salla* the musicians struck up a rhythm to lead the assembly into the streets of Ayia Marina and to the Nikolakis courtyard. Three Kasiot ladies led the march, holding candles before them. Immediately behind them came the musicians, with violin, *laout,* and lyre. Finally, arm in arm came the two male principals in that pageant: the bridegroom, Andoni, and his best man, Dr. Nikolakis.

There were maskers in the streets, out for the first Sunday of the carnivals. White gypsum masks peered out of open doorways. Other inhuman apparitions peered around the corners of dry-stone walls, human bodies with heads of pigs and donkeys. Barefoot children beat stones against tin cans. Other villagers set off fireworks and fired pistols at the sky. And everyone in the procession joined in the call.

"Gambros!" they cried with one voice, as on the Resurrection. *"Gambros!* The bridegroom! *Gambros!"*

At the threshold of the Nikolakis house, Eloula stood with downcast eyes. Beside her stood her matron of honor, Yani's wife, holding the silken quilt she would throw down beneath the feet of the bridegroom as he stepped across the threshold. There was no music now, no pistol shots or fireworks, no shouts of "bridegroom." As Andoni marched arm in arm with his best man, Dr. Nikolakis, Dimitri let go Andoni's arm, allowing the bridegroom to take the final step alone.

Now all Kasos was quiet in anticipation. There was a gentle sound of rain as maidens sprinkled rosewater on the bridegroom's head. Calliope unfurled the silken blanket beneath the bridegroom's feet, and jumping over it and across the threshold, Andoni Manoussos stepped into the courtyard of his bride-to-be.

One week later, Eloula's wedding feast lasted late into the night. By the time the guests had gone, bidding the couple their last good wishes, the spring moon, full as a wineskin, had sunk below the mountains. Now Captain Manoussos and Dr. Nikolakis led the wedding couple to their new house, across the courtyard from the doctor's mother's, and locked the door behind them.

The next day, on thresholds throughout the island, black-cowled prophets mused on the events to come.

"Whatever happens," Sofitsa said, "one of the girls will marry the doctor before this week is out."

"How do you know?" said Kalitsa.

"Simple," said Sofitsa. "Next Sunday is the third

carnival. The Monday after that is Pure Monday. And after Pure Monday, no marriage is permitted until the end of Lent. But the Phillipides and the Yeroyioryis can hardly meet in the street without drawing guns. They'll do anything to settle this affair before Lent begins, and because, according to our religion, the doctor can marry only one of them, *one of them will marry him before this week is out.*"

"I see," said Kalitsa, scratching her head.

The Monday morning after Eloula's wedding, musicians went around the island announcing the doctor's *proxenia* to Marika Yeroyioryis. Then, having made one round, they went around again, announcing his *proxenia* to Fifika Phillipides. In this way, the only double *proxenia* in history sounded over Kasos in a jangled discord.

"What about this Fifika?" said mother Nikolakis. "Why are the musicians announcing that your *proxenia* is concluded to her?"

"Because it is."

"But I've already told you, it is concluded to Marika Yeroyioryis."

"I know. And it is also concluded to Fifika Phillipides."

"But who concluded it?"

"I did."

"You? But why should you do that?"

Dr. Nikolakis explained the impossible, that he had wanted to marry Fifika Phillipides.

"You wanted to marry Fifika Phillipides?" his mother said.

Dimitri nodded.

"And you thought you could just go off and conclude your *proxenia* to her just because you wanted to marry her?"

To this question, Dimitri had no answer. In a dark way, he had been troubled by it himself, though he did not know why.

"So this is my reward after all I've done for you," his mother said. "To see you go off and ask a girl to marry you. Why, her father and her uncles must have fallen off their stools, delighted to get that hussy off their hands."

"She's not a hussy," said Dimitri. "She's a respectful and obedient girl. She is the first daughter of a first daughter, descended in direct lineage from a noble Kasiot family."

"Squashes and cucumbers for her lineage. She must be a hussy, to make you agree to marry her against your will!"

"I did not agree against my will. I agreed on my own accord."

"So much the worse. She must be a witch, to make a man agree to marry her on his own accord."

"You're the one who's trying to make me marry against my will," the doctor said. "You're trying to force me to marry Marika Yeroyioryis."

"Marika Yeroyioryis is not a hussy," said his mother. "She's an obedient and respectful girl, the first daughter of a first daughter, descended from a noble Kasiot family. And what's more, it wasn't her idea to marry you, it was *my* idea. She never would have thought of marrying you, and you would never have thought of marrying her. But you'll marry her all the same, if I have to stand behind you with a gun. You'll marry her and live with her in that house of hers, which you can see from here, right in this village where I can keep an eye on you. And that's all I have to say on the subject of your marriage."

And that was all Dr. Nikolakis had to hear, for he had just become a revolutionary. Could a man be forced to marry against his will? Was it marriage, to kneel before a tyrant, to wed himself to a puppet bride, the crown lowered on his head by the hand of tyranny itself?

Now that Dr. Nikolakis had pronounced his dogma, he knew his course. Of the two daughters, he would marry Fifika Phillipides, as he agreed in the first place. He would marry the girl he wanted, and if it wasn't in keeping with the Kasiot custom, then squashes and cucumbers for the custom.

On Monday night, one week before Pure Monday, Dr. Nikolakis waited for the time when the lights were out in all the houses of the island and the only sounds were stray dogs howling on the mountains and the unending sea washing the iron shore. Then, after midnight, he made his way through the darkened streets, downhill past the cemetery, through the back streets of Phry.

Dimitri Nikolakis knocked on his brother Yani's door. He asked Yani to lead him to the sheepfold in the hills, and with a smile, Yani agreed. Together they rode past the chapel of the Prophet Elias, opposite the town of Arvanitohori, across a huge canyon opening like a lesion in the rock.

And there, in a sheepfold sheltered from the wind, Dimitri found his hiding place.

He swore his brother to secrecy and gave him a message for the Phillipides. Yani was to say the doctor had been called away to cure an epidemic in Karpathos, but he would marry Fifika as soon as he returned. In the meantime, he would hide in the sheepfold until Pure Monday.

He knew that if he tried to marry Fifika Phillipides before Pure Monday, he would risk being shot by the Yeroyioryis. And even in the cause of freedom, he saw no reason to risk his life. After Lent was over, the Yeroyioryis would be calmer, and he could marry Fifika without danger. As soon as the forty days were over, he would marry Fifika without delay.

The next morning, when first the Phillipides and then the Yeroyioryis went to call on him at his mother's house, Dr. Nikolakis, the child of custom and tradition, had vanished forever from the island, and a new Dr. Nikolakis, the partisan of revolution, was hiding somewhere on the island in his place.

In the final hours of the third Carnival Sunday, the two families roamed the villages, and as peace-loving Kasiots trembled before their guns, they upset furniture in *sallas,* turned over pots and cauldrons in cookhouses, ripped out bedding in *moussandras,* all in search of their chimerical Dr. Nikolakis. The Phillipides knew that the doctor could not have gone to Karpathos, for the island steamer had not put into Kasos since before Eloula's wedding. And not one caïque had left the island in the meantime.

And now, at the story's end, Yani played a final role. Yani had found that marriage was not what he had expected. Far from being beautiful, his wife

Calliope really was too short. And far from being cheerful and good-natured, she was as feebleminded as everybody said. Yani discovered, as husbands often do to their dismay, that though the role of bridegroom is the most heroic in the world, the role of husband is a tragicomic one at best, a mere supporting role. And Yani wanted his older brother to share his fate.

When Yani arrived at the sheepfold in the hills, the sun was already down on the third Sunday of the carnivals. There were maskers abroad again: nymphs and centaurs, satyrs and Nereids, and urchins carrying padlocks to leave on unmarried maidens' doors.

The doctor suspected nothing. What should he suspect, for in those waning hours before Pure Monday, there could be no more *emvasmata,* no nuptial table set, now that the time of marriage was sealed away.

"He's sick," said Yani, "old Petros Phillipides. He trembles so, his soul's between his lips."

Taking his bag of medicines, Dr. Nikolakis mounted the mule behind his brother. They rode down from the hills near Arvanitohori, both of them on one saddle. Down they rode to that deserted plain, sharply rutted with volcanic rock, Yani shouting to the mule and striking its haunches with his whip.

Outside the Phillipides house, they dismounted and went the rest of the way on foot. They marched arm in arm down the path toward the courtyard gate. There, as Dr. Nikolakis reached the Phillipides' threshold, Yani let go his arm, leaving him to take the final steps alone. The next moment, crossing the threshold as blithely as a bridegroom, Dr. Nikolakis stepped into the range of a dozen Phillipides' guns.

"What's this?" said Dr. Nikolakis.

"Your wedding," said Captain Markos.

"My wedding? At gunpoint?"

But the doctor received no answer. Captain Markos's handkerchief was stuffed into his mouth. Father Minas stood behind a wedding table, with Phillipides pistols at his back. In front, supported by a cousin on either side, was a fainting girl: Fifika in her wedding gown.

Her wedding portrait was hardly flattering. Her body was limp, her head fallen forward, the coins of her dowry threaded on her breast like chains. They pushed Dr. Nikolakis beside her, his hands bound behind his back. With the handkerchief still in his mouth, Dr. Nikolakis embraced his fate in silence.

Father Minas abridged this service more skillfully than any other in his career. "The servant of God Dimitri is crowned for the handmaiden of God Fifika . . ." he sang. "The handmaiden of God Fifika is crowned for the servant of God Dimitri."

Brother Stavros, the best man, switched the crowns over the couple's head, his pistol gleaming in the moonlight. Dr. Nikolakis was crowned for Fifika and she was crowned for him, and the next moment, a Phillipides pistol thrust suddenly into the small of his back, Father Minas cried out: "Rejoice, O Isaiah . . ."

The priest was prodded forward, as was Dr. Nikolakis behind him. But in her fainting condition, Fifika had to be carried. Her uncles and her cousins lifted her off the ground and moved her like a puppet.

It took a long time for the cumbersome party to circle the table three times, and afterward there were no gifts pinned to Fifika's gown, no *mandinadhas* sung in honor of bride and groom. Solemnly, pistols raised and gleaming in the moonlight, all the Phillipides' kissed the wedding crowns.

They carried Fifika to her new house and pushed Dr. Nikolakis after her. They laid her on the gold-embroidered sheets, lifeless as a corpse. Then, loosening Dr. Nikolakis, they locked the door behind them. Finally, in a most uncustomary procedure, they gathered around the house to peer between the shutters.

Inside, Dr. Nikolakis sat on the sofa looking at Fifika, who was lying on the bed. A few hours earlier, he had been hiding in the hills, plotting how to marry her without being shot by the Yeroyioryis. And now, unexpectedly, he had succeeded. With the fulfillment of his wishes within his reach, Dr. Nikolakis sat on the sofa.

But he was thinking: *Could a man be forced to marry against his will? Could a marriage be forced at gunpoint, the crown lowered on his head by the hand of tyranny itself?*

And that was how Dr. Nikolakis worked his woe, insisting on a principle poignantly inappropriate. That was how the roads to wedlock parted before him once again, and this time he chose revolution, exactly at the wrong time.

For though he had been married at gunpoint, it was not to Marika Yeroyioryis but to Fifika Phillipides. Though the hand of tyranny had held the crowns, it had crowned him in wedlock—of all people—to the girl he wanted. At that point, the wise course, even for a revolutionary, would be to throw down his flag at the maiden's feet and proceed according to the custom.

But there are two kinds of revolutionaries: revisionists, who change their principles according to circumstances, and dogmatists, who cling to their principles no matter what. Dr. Nikolakis was a dogmatist, and like any dogmatist, he could embrace the cause but not the maiden. Like any new recruit in freedom's struggle, Dr. Nikolakis found it easier to raise his flag.

At the shutters, the Phillipides' whispered, "What's he doing?"

"Sitting on the sofa," said Captain Markos. "His arms are folded. He will not approach."

"That's outrageous!" cried the others. "We'll not allow it."

"Very well," said Captain Markos. "But what can we do?"

Meanwhile, in the bower, something very surprising happened. Fifika woke up. She sat straight up in her bed, opened her eyes, and saw the doctor sitting before her. Suddenly, in that one moment, all Dr. Nikolakis's doctrine was undone. Fifika was not a puppet after all! She was a living girl, the one he had chosen as his bride!

And how beautiful she was! Why had he not discovered that before? Her face was white as milk, her black hair falling down around it in perfect ringlets. And those eyes! They rested on him so directly, so personally and intimately. They looked so bewildered, so humble, so noble in their unwillingness to reproach him.

"Why have you done this?" they seemed to ask. "Why do you let them treat me this way?"

A flood of feeling rose in Dimitri Nikolakis's heart. Only a madman would decline to have her! No man in his senses would refuse this maiden for his wife!

He wanted to run to her, to kneel before her, to beg forgiveness. More than anything in the world he wanted her. Finally, Dimitri Nikolakis knew, as he had never known before, that Fifika Phillipides was the girl he wanted for his wife.

But at that moment, at the window, other dogmatists were clamoring in outrage, raising a banner of their own in the face of changing facts.

To an enraptured man in loving contemplation of his bride, they shouted: "We will not stand for that!"

To a bridegroom paralyzed with wonder, gazing on the girl he loved, they shouted: "We'll not permit such outrage!"

The next instant, the Phillipides burst through the windows, firing pistols into the air.

"Out of here," they shouted. "We'll have a husband for our daughter, not a fop!"

Dr. Nikolakis jumped through the window and landed in the courtyard. Fifika, conscious for long enough to see her family come in firing pistols, and her lately married husband depart a moment later, sank into oblivion again.

Around her, the Phillipides danced like demons.

"Gone," said a Phillipides brother at the window, watching Dr. Nikolakis sprint through the gate and out into the streets of Panayia.

"Let him run to hell," shouted another Phillipides. "We'll find another bridegroom for our daughter, and he'll marry her this very night."

He meant, of course, that without consummation, the ceremony was an empty ritual, the crown a hollow crown. They would find another bridegroom to take the doctor's place, and they would find him before the night was done.

Once again they gathered Fifika in their arms and lifted her from her wedding bed. They mounted mules, and carried her on their shoulders, like a corpse in bridal clothes.

Meanwhile, Dr. Nikolakis had taken the other road off toward Ayia Marina. Maskers along the way stood aside for him—Turkish pashas, Jews in pillowed pantaloons, satyrs, nymphs, centaurs—all made way for the strangest creature abroad that night, a bridegroom running from his wedding bed.

Dimitri held his pace uphill, up the road beyond the Bucca, past carob and olive branches gleaming in the moonlight in gloomy ecstasy. Then he came upon a band of maskers who would not make way.

He didn't see them until he had run straight into their midst. There were a dozen bandits, shouting and waving pistols. Among them was a priest, and beside him, seated on a mule, was a young woman in bridal clothes: Marika Yeroyioryis.

"We've been expecting you, Dr. Nikolakis," said Captain Manoli. "We wonder what custom you can conjure now to prevent your marrying our daughter."

"A simple one," said Dr. Nikolakis. "I'm married."

"Married?" said Captain Manoli.

"Married," said Dr. Nikolakis. "To Fifika Phillipides. My regrets, gentlemen. A previous engagement, you understand."

"On the contrary," said Captain Manoli, thinking quickly, speaking now not only to Dr. Nikolakis, but to the audience of the island and all posterity as well. "We must offer our regrets to *you*. We are embarrassed to meet you here, as technically your *proxenia* was concluded to our daughter. But I tell you frankly, when you stopped us now, we were on our way to our daughter's wedding. She will be married this very night to another."

"Then long life to her," said Dr. Nikolakis.

"And long life to you," said Captain Manoli Yeroyioryis.

And so the Yeroyioryis took their leave of Dr. Nikolakis for the last time. Dragging their helpless daughter after them, and Papa Minas to his second wedding of the evening, they descended to the town of Phry.

The Yeroyioryis were the first to reach the café above the Bucca. (The Phillipides spent time searching for Papa Minas.) There, above that placid bowl, a rowdy symposium had lasted late into the night. Two roistering philosophers, Pavlos the tailor and Kosta the cobbler—both of them in their forties and still unmarried—were discussing the subject of the day.

"I'd rather never marry," Pavlos said, "than sell my heart for a house and dowry. Pavlos the tailor will wait for love."

"And what will you do with it?" said Kosta the cobbler. "Can you eat it? Will you wear it? One girl is as good as another and even the gorgon has her charms. But the reason I have never married and probably never shall is that I've never heard of a dowry large enough to tempt me."

"And how much would be required?" said a man at the head of a large party riding mules right up to the café. "How much would be required to tempt you with the hand of Marika Yeroyioryis?"

"Marika Yeroyioryis?" laughed the cobbler. "The one who is engaged to Dr. Nikolakis? And who is offering her hand to me?"

"Her *father*," said the newcomer, pointing his pistol at the cobbler. "And as for your Dr. Nikolakis, such a girl as my Marika is beyond his wildest dreams."

"Well, well," said the cobbler. "Then I must beg your pardon. But if she is beyond a doctor's dreams, she must be beyond my dreams as well, for I am but a poor cobbler, and at this moment, a drunken one."

"A cobbler is an honest trade," said Captain Manoli, "and being drunk is not a disadvantage. Once you are a husband, you won't take long to sober up."

The cobbler scratched his head and understood that it was not simply his imagination, that it was really Marika Yeroyioryis bound to the mule beside her father, and that her father was actually offering him her hand.

"In that case," he said slyly, "how much is offered?"

"A hundred sovereigns," said the captain, "and all her mills and fields."

"Only a hundred?" said the cobbler. "They say the doctor was offered five hundred and he refused."

"From the Phillipides!" roared the captain. "With such a prospect as their daughter, they had to borrow money to get her off their hands. From the Yeroyioryis, the doctor was offered nothing."

"I must consider," said the cobbler, smirking. "For a hundred sovereigns, I need time to think."

"Then you have twenty seconds," replied the captain, pointing the pistol at the cobbler's head.

"Twenty seconds? And after that, what then?"

"You will be shot.

"Well, in that case, I need no more time. For a hundred sovereigns, I agree."

"Agreed!" shouted Captain Manoli.

"Agreed!" shouted all the Yeroyioryis and the drunken elders of the Bucca.

Papa Minas performed the service. Marika Yeroyioryis, fainting on her mule, was crowned for Kosta the cobbler, and he was crowned for her.

"Shameful!" said Pavlos, on his dogma. "Pavlos the tailor will wait for love."

"Then wait no longer," said another newcomer, leading another mounted party to the café. "Love is here."

This time, the priest thought he had gone mad. He thought he had fallen under a curse always to be haunted by these fanatical families. First he must marry off Fifika, then Marika; then, at last after he married off Marika, here was Fifika once again.

"Here she is," the Phillipides shouted, handing down their daughter. "Here is the girl you have waited for. You are the bridegroom for our Fifika. You are her *gambros*."

"*Gambros!*" said the Yeroyioryis', and they too

believed they were seeing ghosts. "Your daughter has no *gambros?*"

"Not now, but she is soon to have him," said Captain Markos. "She is about to marry Pavlos the tailor."

"But what about Dr. Nikolakis?" said Captain Manoli. "He was married to your daughter this very night."

"In his dreams, perhaps," said Captain Markos. "Pavlos the tailor, do you agree to marry this girl, with a hundred sovereigns to accompany her hand?"

"Agreed," said Pavlos.

And that is how two noble Kasiot daughters, two princesses of the island, were given away, one to a cobbler, the other to a tailor. And that is how two Kasiot sophists, less subtle than Dr. Nikolakis, won the prizes he had lost, for they understood, as the doctor did not, that freedom has nothing to do with marriage in any case, and if a man is out to consummate a wedding, the flag of freedom must come down and some kneeling before the tyrant must be done.

After the final bride departed, Dimitri Nikolakis sat down by the dry-stone wall. The next morning he would return to Ayia Marina, to live with his mother and fulfill the prophecy she had so often recited in golden tones, that there was no girl on Kasos worthy to become his bride.

But that night, he slept beside the dry-stone wall, beside a prickly pear as contorted as a bridegroom's road to marriage, beneath a humpbacked olive gossiping in the wind. And the next morning, when Pure Monday dawned and urchins smirked to see the mischief of the night before, Dr. Nikolakis awoke beside

the dry-stone wall, his arms folded on his breast, and
a large paper padlock fastened around his neck.

The R & K partners. Seated from left: Manuel
Kulukundis, Minas Rethymnis, Basil Mavroleon.
Standing from right: my father Michael Kulukundis,
Uncle George, Uncle Nicholas, Uncle John.

BLACK BIRD, GREEK
FLAG OVER KASOS

*T*he island is like me, and the island's life is like my life. I went to Greece as a toddler in 1939 and spent almost a year in Syros. Throughout my childhood, people told me how I used to sit on the terrace and pretend I was on the bridge of a sailing ship, how I used to ride on my grandfather's shoulders and speak Greek in the heavy accent of the waterfront. But despite what people told me, I could remember nothing for myself. My first memory of life was that hotel room in Westchester and the arabesques on the carpet.

In the same way, in some remote era of the past, Kasos was a Hellenic island. But the island knew nothing of this former life. The only Greece it could believe in was the Greece it knew. When Kasos awoke to memory, it was a subject people in a foreign nation, born in *xenitia*.

The first people known to have stood on Kasos were Phoenicians. They were the ones who gave the island its name: Kas, the island of sea-foam. The island is mentioned in Homer's ship list of the *Iliad,* Hellenized as Kasos. Later it was settled by the Dorians at about the time they settled Rhodes, Kos, and Crete.

During the classical period, the city was on the site of the present town of Poli (the name itself means city) on a steep slope at the southeastern corner of the plateau. There, in 1847, the German archaeologist Ludwig Ross found the remnants of an ancient wall and the fragments of a statue, probably of Apollo.

The ancient harbor Imborio (meaning trade or commerce) was a small cove below the site of Poli. Up to the end of the nineteenth century, a shipbuilding yard was located there.

By the end of the first century of the Christian era, Kasos, along with the rest of Greece, was a part of the Roman Empire. In A.D. 330, when the empire moved to Byzantium, Kasos came under the rule of the emperor on the Bosporus. The Bishop of Karpathos and Kasos attended the first Ecumenical Council in Nicaea in A.D. 325. Because of its geographical position, Kasos must have done a fair trade, and like Rhodes and its other neighbors, it must have been densely populated.

But time was to take its toll on Kasos, as did the geographical position that helped it prosper. In the seventh century a wave of invasion curled out of Arabia, and like its neighbors Crete and Karpathos, Kasos became an outpost for Arab pirates.

In 961, the Byzantines reconquered it, but in the succeeding centuries the sun began to set on the Eastern Empire. In 1204, the western Roman Catholic knights of the Fourth Crusade turned from their stated destination of Jerusalem and attacked the emperor at Constantinople. On that day, hated in the Romaic world forever after, the ancient city of Constantinople was sacked. A western ruler, Baldwin of Flanders, sat on the Byzantine throne, and the Romaic lands were divided among the western princes.

In the meantime, a darker day was about to dawn. On a black Tuesday in 1453, the Ottoman Turks conquered the ancient Byzantine capital. The citizens of the empire were reduced to the status of a subject people, known to their masters as Romaioi, their language as Romaic.

In their heyday, the Ottoman Turks carried the crescent into Belgrade and Budapest, and even the princes of western Europe dreaded their advance. Headed by the renowned Admiral Barbarossa, the Ottoman fleet conquered most of the Archipelago. The Venetians, who had occupied Kasos in the meantime, were driven out and forced to take refuge in Crete. From that year onward, like most of Greece, Kasos became part of the Ottoman Empire.

The succeeding centuries brought little change to Kasos as they brought little change to Greece. The Turks and Venetians waged a continual battle for the Romaic lands, and the Greeks participated in the struggle as galley slaves, fighting on both sides, killing each other in the service of others. As a political people, the Greeks did not exist.

But Kasos's very poverty saved it from the brunt of Turkish tyranny. Sultan Suleiman, who conquered the Dodecanese, saw little purpose in ruling the Twelve Islands, of which Kasos was one. Instead, he granted them certain privileges, later confirmed by successive sultans throughout the centuries.

Except for Rhodes and Kos, which were fertile and populous enough to make a stricter rule worthwhile, the islands were to have no Turkish governors. Their citizens were not to be subject to induction in the Turkish armies, and their only obligation was to pay a yearly tax, according to the size of their population. The islanders were to collect this tax—no Turkish officials were allowed to interfere—and in all other matters the islanders were to rule themselves.

But despite this freedom from oppression, rocky islands with no shelter from the sea could offer little protection for their inhabitants. The inhabitants built their villages at the interior of the plateau, as far from the sea as possible, but throughout the fifteenth and sixteenth centuries, when piracy in the Aegean was at its height, Kasiot homes were never safe from plunder. Kasiots themselves were constantly being carried off to the slave markets of Asia Minor and North Africa. During these centuries, the population of the island was steadily depleted, until finally, at the end of the sixteenth century, travelers passing by the island found it uninhabited.

In this period Kasos was actually severed from its past. Bald and solitary as an infant, it was carried mindlessly upon the sea. During that time it was probably resettled by Albanians. A village at the interior of the plateau named Arvanitohori (Albanian-Town) was founded in this period. In addition, there must have been non-Albanians living there at the time, probably Cretans fleeing the persecution of both

Venetians and Turks. Otherwise, why should Albanians name it Albanian-Town?

Meanwhile, the mind of Kasos slept on, not remembering. No light fell upon the island, just as before the dawn of memory, no light falls upon the infant's mind. In those dark, uninhabited decades, Kasos was a phantom island, sailing on an unremembered sea.

The miracle is that when it emerged at last, Kasos was Greek: the miracle of heredity itself. Not only is there no Albanian spoken on Kasos today, in Arvanitohori or any other village, but none of the languages of its other erstwhile masters is spoken either: no Turkish, Arabic, or Italian, except those elements that have been assimilated into Greek.

In addition, there are other strong traces of the island's Hellenism, preserved unconsciously. They are implicit in naming and inheritance customs, in rites of grieving, in a cult of vengeance, in casual references to Charon, the Fates, and other pagan deities heard in Kasos to this day.

In 1788, a light was turned on Kasos, and suddenly the island was revealed. The French philosopher Claude Savary, bound for Crete, met adverse winds and was forced to seek refuge on a barren island thirty miles from his destination. He spent about a week there, waiting for calmer weather. During that time he wrote a letter describing his accidental visit, which was included in his volume *Letters on Greece,* published in 1788.

"The boat was let down," he wrote, "but we knew not where to land. All over the coast we could discover nothing but threatening pointed rocks against which the waves broke with a bellowing noise, whitening them with foam."

Here indeed was the Phoenicians' Kas, the island of sea-foam.

One of the inhabitants came down to the shore and waved a handkerchief near a place where Savary could land. It was the Bucca, which exists today: a small harbor, sealed off from the sea by two breakwaters.

Today the Bucca is surrounded by the town of Phry, a placid bowl beneath the bell tower with the clock. But in those days there was no town and no bell tower. (Phry was built in the 1830s to house the refugees returning to Kasos after the revolution.) In 1788 the plain around the Bucca was empty, and from the higher ground, four Kasiot villages peered at the approaching strangers.

But the French flag flying in the lee of Makra Island must have relieved the Kasiots. Trusting that these men approaching the Bucca meant no harm, an anonymous Kasiot came down to meet them, not realizing quite another possibility: that this was not a piratical but a historical adventure. Waving his handkerchief in all ingenuousness, he beckoned the discoverer to wrest his island from its secure oblivion.

The entrance to the Bucca was no more than a dozen feet wide, no wider than it is today. To enter it, a boat must proceed cautiously, through the middle of the opening, with no room around it even for the oars to be extended. As Savary's boat advanced, a violent surge rose suddenly, threatening to dash the boat against the rocks.

The Kasiot called one of his countrymen, and the two of them stood, one on either side of the opening, signaling to Savary's men to push forward with the oars. At the instant the boat entered the treacherous pass, they held it off with long poles and guided it into the harbor.

In that way, Kasos was discovered. In the person of this lucky Frenchman, Kasos made connection with its future. For the first time in history, a recording eye was turned upon the island, and from Savary's description, we see an island we can recognize:

> Below the hill from which I made my observations, stands a small chapel surrounded by fig-trees. Here begin a chain of hills that, bending into a semi-circle, leave in the middle a plain of a league in circumference, which has been cleared out by the inhabitants, with infinite labor.
>
> They have torn up large pieces of rock, and removed heaps of stones, with which they have formed the walls of the enclosure. All this space is divided into compartments and shared among the Kasiots. They sow barley and wheat.
>
> The sides of the hills are covered with vineyards, the grapes of which produce a very agreeable wine. I could not help admiring the industry with which these islanders have been able to cultivate rocks, hardly covered with a few inches of earth . . .

Savary found the eating habits different from those
in Paris: the men dining in a circle on the carpet, the
women in a separate room. For dinner that evening,
Savary ate pullet with rice, fresh eggs, pigeons, cheese,
and wine. After dinner there was a dance.

About twenty young girls, dressed all in
white, with flowing robes, and plaited locks,
entered the apartment, and with them a young
man who played on the lyre, which he
accompanied with his voice. Several of them
were handsome, all healthy and lively . . .

The uniform dress of these nymphs, the
modesty which heightened their charms, their
becoming bashfulness, their joyous but decent
merriment, all contributed to make me almost
imagine myself suddenly transported to the
island of Calypso.

They began to range themselves in a ring,
and invited me to dance. I did not wait for
many entreaties. The circle we formed is sin-
gular from the manner in which it is inter-
woven: the dancer does not give his hand to
the two persons next him, but to those next
them, so that you can have your hands crossed
before your neighbors, who are thus locked,
as it were, in the links of a double chain.

This interweaving is not without pleasure,
for reasons by no means difficult to understand. In the middle of the circle stood the
musician, who played and sang at the same
time, while all he dancers kept exact time . . .
For myself, I followed where my partners led

me, my mind being less occupied with the dance than with the charming females who composed it. [Author's note: The dance was the *Foumisto,* traditionally danced at weddings, but apparently also on special occasions, such as the arrival of a Frenchman.]

Savary's host, eager for him to take away a good report of the island, showed him letters written by two provençal captains landed on Kasos before him. The Kasiot could not read French, but he knew they must be testimonials to his native island, and valuing them among his most precious possessions, he kept them locked up in a coffer. Proudly, he brought them out and unrolled them.

The first one read: "Frenchmen whom the tempest may throw upon this island, confide in the inhabitants: I was shipwrecked on these rocks, and they afforded me every succour that men owe each other in similar misfortunes."

The second one read: "I warn such of my countrymen as chance may bring [to Kasos] to be upon their guard and put no confidence in the inhabitants. They are a set of thieves and knaves and strangers have everything to apprehend from their rapacity."

Looking up at his host, Savary saw him beaming with pleasure, and so he returned the letters to him, saying only that he needed no testimonials to rely on his integrity. The Kasiot smiled in great satisfaction and locked up his treasure once again.

For his part, Savary did well by Kasos. He was a Frenchman in the tradition of Rousseau, and what he found on Kasos suited him. He wrote:

Happy people, ambition and intrigue trouble not your tranquility; the thirst of gold hath not corrupted your manners; the quarrels, dissensions, and crimes with which it hath covered the earth are to you unknown. Here, no citizen, proud of his titles, or his wealth, tramples under foot his humble countrymen; no cringing valet flatters the vices of his master; man is equal to man, nor does the Kasiot blush, or abase himself before the Kasiot.

Before Savary's generation—and the French Revolution—passed into history, the Greek Revolution had begun. Kasiots stood to gain very little from it, as their privileges already granted them almost complete freedom. But freedom meant not only deliverance from oppression but national identity as well. For that reason, however free from oppression the Kasiots may have been in 1821, they were as eager to embrace the cause of revolution as though they had been suffering under the tyrant's heel.

A Kasiot captain, Grigoriades, was on his way from Smyrna to Syros with Moslem passengers on board when news of the revolution reached him. Suddenly, he changed course and sailed for Kasos. There, anchoring in full view of the Kasiot population, he brought all the Moslem passengers on deck and cut their throats.

As he declared boastfully sometime later, he wanted to share Moslem blood with Kasos, to stain it indelibly with revolution, to bind its destiny with the cause of Greece.

But the Kasiots did not need such a spectacle to stir them. Immediately, they put to sea, armed with guns and ammunition bought or stolen from neutral ships. At home, a population of thirty-five hundred prepared for war.

In the previous decade, the increased trade in the Mediterranean of the Napoleonic Wars enabled several Greek islands—Hydra, Spetsai, Psara, and Kasos—to develop powerful merchant fleets.

At the time, the Hydriots had a hundred and fifteen ships larger than a hundred tons, the Spetsiots sixty, the Psariots forty, and the Kasiots fifteen. The Greek revolutionaries formed a central treasury and began to levy taxes, and the Hydriots, as the largest naval power, were authorized to dispense the proceeds and assume command over Greek naval operations.

For some reason lost to history, the Hydriots decided that the Kasiots should not be full-fledged members of the Revolutionary Navy, and if the Kasiots wished to sail with the ships of the other three naval islands, they must do so at their own expense.

For a time, the Kasiots did so. Then, because they feared an attack upon their island, more remote and exposed to the enemy than Hydra and Spetsai, they returned to protect it.

Thereafter, the Kasiots acted on their own, harassing the Turkish and Egyptian supply lines in the Eastern Mediterranean. When the Cretans rose, Kasiot ships assisted in the sieges of the fortresses of Khania, Suda, and Rethymnon along the northern coast.

They also set up a blockade of Crete, intercepting all ships, including those of neutral powers, with cargoes intended for the Turks. In Damietta, on the coast of Syria, four Kasiot captains surprised thirteen vessels loaded with rice for the sultan's fleet, one of them containing one million piastres in cash. Seizing three ships, they filled them with the piastres and as much booty as they would hold, and towed them off for Kasos.

The sultan could not bear such outrages for long. In 1823, his Egyptian viceroy, Mohammed Ali, entered the war and sent his son, Ibrahim Pasha, to put down the revolt in Crete. By the beginning of 1824, the fires in Crete had been reduced to embers. Much of the population fled the island, many in Kasiot ships; and an estimated twenty-five hundred had taken refuge in Kasos.

Now, in 1824, Ibrahim was preparing to invade the Peloponnese. But before he could embark on an invasion, he needed a base in Crete and supply lines from Egypt. To make these secure, he had to break the power of a barren island thirty miles from Crete's eastern tip.

So the beginning of 1824 boded ominously for Kasos.

The Kasiots wrote to Hydra, begging for the fleet to come to their assistance. If they could resist Ibrahim's invasion, the Egyptians' entire northward advance would be delayed. But the Hydriots replied that they could not dispatch the fleet until a loan arrived from England, as the sailors would not go to sea without wages.

Again, the Hydriot motives are obscure. There

must have been plenty of money in the treasury to pay the sailors, and true patriots will sail without wages if necessary. Probably the Hydriots were preoccupied with the feuding then going on among the Greek leaders.

So Kasos was left alone with her destiny. Instead of transporting the population to the mainland, the captains felt they must defend their homes in the face of danger. And they believed their surest chance against the overwhelming odds would be to make their defense on land.

The ironbound coast of Kasos afforded no easy access, and the Kasiots believed if they could fortify the three miles across the opening of the plateau, the rest of the island would be impregnable. Accordingly, they disarmed their ships and anchored them at Imborio.

They erected a battery of some thirty guns across the mouth of the plateau, spaced out behind a rampart extending from Imborio in the east to St. George of the Spring in the west. Behind the rampart, five hundred Kasiots took their places with five hundred Cretans. Behind them, in the four villages that had peered down at Savary, an unarmed population grown to 5,000 waited in their houses.

The Egyptian fleet appeared under forty-five sail, transporting a troop of three to four thousand Albanians under the command of Hussein Bey. It tried one assault, which proved unsuccessful. And there are two widely differing explanations of what happened next.

According to the Kasiot version, the Egyptians opened fire on their first attack, and, unable to bring the island to submission, they steered directly for the open land at the opening of the plateau and attempted an invasion.

But Kasiot resistance proved too strong for them. The Egyptians gave way and sailed off for Rhodes. And there, to the island's everlasting grief, they found a Kasiot named Zacharias, exiled from his native island for immoral behavior. On the night of June 7, by the old calendar, he returned to Kasos with the Egyptian fleet, and—compounding immorality with treason—he showed them a secret cleft in the iron coast, a fatal landing place beyond the range of the thirty guns.

The second version comes from Alexandria, in an anonymous letter to the British Ambassador at Constantinople. Because it comes originally from Egypt, it must be the version the Egyptian fleet brought home. According to this report, as the Egyptian warships advanced upon the island, the flag-ship *Diana* struck a reef, opening a large hole in her side. Shipping water rapidly, the *Diana* turned from battle and, thinking she was leading a retreat, the other Egyptian warships turned from battle after her.

The fleet sailed away to repair the damage, in the direction of Rhodes. They found a harbor, probably in Karpathos, and anchored there until the *Diana* could repair her hull. This done, they returned to Kasos and sacked the island.

Kasiot though I am, I confess I incline to the second version. I can hardly believe that the Egyptians could have found a lone Kasiot exile among the population of Rhodes. How would he have known that they were planning an attack on Kasos, and so come down to the harbor to volunteer his services? According to the legend, Zacharias killed himself during the invasion, but his body was not found afterward by the surviving population, as it surely would have been to be decorated in ways appropriate to a traitor.

Finally, the cleft in the Kasiot coast could not have been a secret. It was a strip of beach called Antiperatos, which exists today just west of where the rampart would have ended. It was plainly visible on our arrival, so that when the Egyptians approached the island from the same direction, they would surely have seen it. The Kasiot defenses seemed naïve to them: a rampart studiously guarding the mouth of the plateau, when beyond it an unprotected landing site afforded easy access.

But although the Kasiot defenses did not prove invincible, the Kasiot imagination did. The Spartans at Thermopylae also held the pass against overwhelming odds, until a traitor showed the enemy a secret cleft between the mountains. Two millennia later, the story of the fall of Kasos is so similar, it seems likely that the Kasiots used the earlier tale to explain their catastrophe.

Except for Zacharias, the two versions agree.

June 7 was a dark night. Anchoring off Kasos a second time, the Egyptians sent eighteen landing craft in an apparent attempt to land before the thirty guns.

While this landing occupied the Kasiots' attention, thirty more landing craft crept up the shore to Antiperatos, the beach beyond the battery. There the invaders surprised four Kasiot guards and slew them without a sound.

From then on, the island's doom was sealed. Three thousand Albanians crept up the slope to Ayia Marina and took instant possession of the village. From that point, the highest habitable vantage place, they must have seen exactly the same sight that had greeted Savary thirty-eight years earlier: a plateau of a league in circumference and several villages facing north.

Some Kasiots fled and hid in caves and others escaped in small boats, sailing miraculously through the Egyptian fleet. Hussein hoped to take as many prisoners as possible, to impress them into service on Ismael's ships; before attacking, he gave the Kasiots a chance to surrender.

But when the remaining Kasiots refused his offer, Ismael's patience was at an end, and he gave the order to attack. The Albanians laid waste the island, burning and pillaging. They killed a total of five hundred Kasiots and Cretans, and impressed the rest as sailors in the Egyptian navy. They burned the ships standing on the ways, and towed all those anchored at Imborio back to Crete. When they departed, they took two thousand Kasiot women and children as slaves to be sold in the markets of Smyrna and Alexandria.

When the Hydriot ships arrived at last, they found a ghost of Kasos. Skeletons of houses stared at their arrival, and the only visible sign of life was a black bird making wide circles overhead.

From that time onward, Kasos performed no service for the revolution. It lost its people to *xenitia,* some to destitution on other islands, others to a harsher fate as slaves. The island itself was as barren as it had been in the sixteenth century.

In the meantime, the revolution had come to its successful end. In 1827, in Navarino Bay, the united ships of the English, French, and Russians destroyed the Turkish fleet, and following that decisive victory, Greece came into existence as a new nation.

The problem, from Kasos's point of view, was that it was not included in this nation. It was part of the first agreement of 1829, but then in an afterthought, in the London Protocol of 1830, it was left out. The island of Euboea, which had been Turkish, was awarded to Greece, while Kasos and the rest of the Dodecanese, which had been Greek, were returned to Turkey.

So the island itself had a false arrival. As other Greek lands and islands arrived at their journey's end—Syros among them—Kasos reached a way station, a vantage point from which another journey extended, to a future that could only be imagined beyond a remaining expanse of time and sea.

When people think of ancient Hellas, they do not realize that as a modern nation, Greece is younger than the United States. The result of the revolution was a fraction of present Greece: the Peloponnese, a small corridor of the mainland, and a few Aegean islands in the neighborhood of Syros. Many other lands and islands were left out of the new nation, including Kasos.

For more than a century, Greece pursued her destiny, redeeming her lost children. In 1864 she acquired the Seven Islands of the Ionian; in 1881, Thessaly; Crete in 1912; in 1913, portions of Macedonia and Epirus, the islands of Samos, Chios, Lesbos, and others in the north Aegean. At last, in 1948, she redeemed the final islands: a group lying between Crete and Turkey, called the Dodecanese, or Twelve Islands, among them Kasos.

Since the founding of the Eastern Roman Empire in 330 A.D., Kasos was ruled by Arabs, Venetians, Turks, Russians, Turks again, and finally Italians. With its neighbor Karpathos, it has been under non-Greek rule longer than any other portion of present Greece. Since 1306, it has been Greek for fifty-five years, from 1948 to the time of this writing. With the other islands of the Dodecanese, it is the youngest of Greece's children, the last to be redeemed.

Throughout the nineteenth century, Kasos's *xenitia* was more bitter than ever. There was a Greece beginning at the Gulf of Arta and extending southeast across the Cyclades. But farther south and east, beyond the enchanted boundary, Kasos was a remote province of the Ottoman Empire, a mercantile and cultural backwater. Her children began to abandon her, sailing off into *xenitia*.

Some sailed north to Syros, which had become the metropolis of the Archipelago. At the end of the eighteenth century, Syros had hardly a thousand people, most of them Uniates or Eastern Rite Roman Catholics, descended from the days when the island was Venetian and known as Syra. Like other Catholic islands, Syros remained neutral, paying taxes both to the revolutionaries and to the Turks. And because of this neutrality, Syros became the refuge for many Greeks from other islands. By the end of the Revolution its population had grown to forty thousand.

Like my grandfather's grandfather, Kasiots sailed to Syros to register their ships with the Greek authorities and gain the right to fly the Greek flag. Many of them stayed on, to educate their children in Greek schools or simply for the privilege of living in Greece. At the same time, Kasiots began to emigrate southward.

Ferdinand de Lesseps founded the Suez Canal Company, and eight years later, six thousand Kasiots were living and working near the isthmus. Throughout the nineteenth century, the emigrations continued, to Africa and Australia, to Canada and the United States.

Meanwhile, on the island, the sultan reaffirmed Kasos's ancient privileges, and the island maintained its system of self-government. Its ruling body was a group of elders known as the *Demogerontia*, representing each of the villages, elected annually by the entire population of the island.

This body collected the tax and otherwise regulated the civil and commercial life of the island. Disputes were settled according to local customs, which were strict though unwritten, and interpreted always by the elders. In addition, there was an ecclesiastical court to decide questions relating to dowry or inheritance and other spiritual matters. Finally, there was a political court, which tried minor criminal cases. The few major crimes in the history of the island were tried in Rhodes.

In 1867 there was a revolution in Crete, and the incorrigible Kasiots sent men to support it. As a result, the sultan decided that Kasos and the rest of the Dodecanese must each have a Turkish *kaimakami,* or governor, to keep a watch on the islanders' activities. Nevertheless, this *kaimakami* could not interfere with the work of the *Demogerontia.* He intruded so little into the life of the island that Aphrodite remembered that he said good morning to the islanders in Greek.

In 1908, the Young Turks overthrew the sultan and tried to rescind the Dodecanese's privileges. They devised an administration for the islands and proposed to levy increased taxes. But the Young Turks had no time to put these intentions into practice. The Dodecanese was about to be taken from them, and the final, darkest chapter of Kasos's exile was about to begin.

In 1912 the Balkan Wars broke out, and by 1913, when the last peace treaty was signed, Greece had achieved the greatest territorial expansion in her history.

Once again, as in the early years of the revolution, the Greek fleet sailed supreme in the Aegean, liberating islands one by one. In a single year, Chios, Samos, Lesbos, Lemnos, Samothrace, and Thasos all became Greek. If the Greek fleet had been able to sail into the Dodecanese, it too could have been liberated.

But in 1911, Italy had gone to war with Turkey over Cyrenaica and Tripolitania on the North African coast, and as a strategic maneuver she sent her fleet to occupy the Dodecanese, so the Italian fleet was already there. To the Greek islanders they posed as liberators. The Italian commanding general declared: "After the termination of the Italo-Turkish War, these islands, temporarily occupied by Italy, will receive an autonomous system of government . . . and the Turk will return no more. This I say as a general and as a Christian, and you should believe my words as words of the gospel."

The islanders called a congress of delegates on the island of Patmos to draft a resolution and laws for the self-government of the Dodecanese. After hearing a liturgy in the cave of St. John the Evangelist, the delegates issued a proclamation of autonomy. They named the new island nation The Aegean State, established the laws of Greece and customs of each local community as the law of the land, and declared their wish for *enosis,* or union with Greece. Poignantly enough, they even devised a provisional flag to fly over the islands until the Greek flag could be raised: a blue field with a white cross and a portrait of Apollo.

But the Dodecanesians were soon to realize that, like the gospel, the Italian general's words were open to different interpretations. What followed was a tortuous road through the subtleties of Italian diplomacy, and they were to emerge not in the autonomous state they originally envisaged, but under the fascist government of Mussolini.

By the Treaty of Lausanne of 1912, the Turks were to evacuate Tripolitania and the Italians were to evacuate the Dodecanese. But neither party observed the treaty. While matters stood in this uncertain state, World War I broke out. After remaining neutral at the beginning, Italy declared war on the Central Powers in 1915. The secret price for this allegiance, agreed upon in London, was that Italy could keep the Dodecanese.

In the meantime, under Mussolini, a fascist government was set up for the Dodecanese that did not feel bound to honor the ancient privileges granted by the Turks. By decree in 1924, the Italian governor-general of the Dodecanese kept all powers of a commander in a military occupation.

Sub-governors were appointed to rule groups of islands under him, while a marshal and a detachment of *carabinieri* were posted on each individual island. In all respects, the autonomy of the islanders was a dead letter. The Demogerontia still collected taxes, but now there was no limit as had existed under the Turks.

The islanders could still elect their *demogeronts,* but they did so from an approved slate of candidates. Legally, the islanders were considered Italian subjects and not Italian citizens, a distinction that provided the rationale for most of the violations of their civil rights. The road to power and privilege was open to them only if they became Italian citizens, and to do so, they had to join the Fascist Party.

Otherwise, the islanders had no civil rights. They could be sent into exile by decree, or moved about from one island to another. They could not travel abroad without permission, and their property could be confiscated to be used in the construction of military bases and tourist hotels or awarded to settlers arrived from Italy. Their businesses were eventually suppressed, including the sponge-fishing industry, which had thrived on Symi and Kalimnos. (During that period, Symiots and Kalimniots founded the large sponge-fishing community that exists today in Tarpon Springs, Florida.)

But in ruling the Dodecanese, the Italians made two mistakes that the Turks had scrupulously avoided. They attacked Greek culture and the Orthodox religion. National demonstrations were forbidden. Greek holidays had to pass unobserved. No Greek flag was to be flown anywhere in the Dodecanese and no houses or churches could be painted blue and white. (By some oversight, the house with the blue shutters miraculously survived on Kasos.)

The authorities made the study of Italian compulsory in the island schools, and they required all instruction to be in Italian. Greek was studied only as a foreign language.

In the first year of the new policy, school enrollment dropped sharply. Before long, most of the Dodecanesian schools were closed. Some students received instruction secretly from tutors, but most of them simply remained uneducated, a loss they had later to repair as well as they could.

The attack on the Orthodox religion was more devious. The Italians attempted to detach the Dodecanesian Church from the Ecumenical Patriarchate at Istanbul by making it *autocephalous* or independent.

Apostolos, the Metropolitan of Rhodes, was the key figure in the plan, and in 1921 the Italian government banished him to Patmos and kept him there for three years.

In 1924 he was released from Patmos and promptly applied for *autocephalous* status for his church, entering into a complicity that made him anathema to his spiritual children. The Patriarch replied that he would grant the request only if a plebiscite were held in the Dodecanese to determine the will of the people. The plebiscite was never held.

In the meantime, the Italian government attempted to achieve its ends *de facto*. Orthodox priests and bishops were forced to resign, and Uniates were appointed in their places. Those Orthodox who objected were imprisoned, and soon the island jails were full of beards and robes.

The islanders responded to any innovation in their religion by rioting. When a Catholic wafer was substituted for the wine of the Orthodox communion, the result was bloodshed at the altar. Ultimately, the islanders preserved their freedom of religion the same way as they did their language. If they could not hear an Orthodox liturgy, they would not go to church. In a short time, most of the island churches were closed, and those churches where Uniates presided were empty. Until the Italians departed from the islands, Dodecanesians held their marriages, christened their children, and buried their dead with secret rites.

This is a story not of oppression, but of exile, the story of the *xenitia* of an island and a people. There is one point about Italian rule that pertains to our story. In 1912, when the Italians arrived, the population of the Dodecanese was 143,000. In 1944, when they left, it was 100,000.

On those islands more prone to emigration by a tradition of seafaring, the discrepancy was more dramatic. In 1912, the population of Symi was 23,000; in 1944, it was 2,000. In 1912, the population of Kasos was 7,000; in 1944, it was 900.

The rest of the story is the story of the Second World War. By 1936, there were thirty-five Italian warships and two hundred Italian planes harbored in the Dodecanese. In addition to garrisons and airfields, the Italians built submarine stations and an airbase on Leros, under hundreds of feet of rock, where planes could take off and be in the air before they emerged from shelter.

Italian troops passed through the islands every week on their way to Ethiopia, then stopped on their way back, to rid themselves of malaria before being transported back to Italy.

In October 1940, in the wake of Hitler's successive victories, Mussolini delivered an ultimatum to Greece to submit within three hours. The answer was the famous "No!" heralding an astounding upset in which the Greek army, with British support, not only expelled the Italian invasion but also advanced into Albania, where the Italians had been entrenched.

Meanwhile, in the Aegean, after being routed by the British fleet off Cape Mattapan, the Italian fleet withdrew harmlessly into its Dodecanesian harbors, leaving the British to cruise the Archipelago at will.

Hitler came to Mussolini's aid, and in April 1941 the German army crossed the Greek border, proceeded down the Vardar River, and broke the line of Greek resistance. The Greek army capitulated; and the Greek government escaped to Egypt. In the meantime, the British Expeditionary Force withdrew, and Greece came under military occupation.

For the next two years, the two Axis Powers divided control of the nation between them. The

Germans ruled Crete and most of the mainland, while the Italians added most of the islands of the Archipelago to their command at Rhodes. Then, in 1943, Italy surrendered to the Allies.

Now, in this final chapter of the island's exile, the expatriated islanders had their chance to play a role. The battle for the Dodecanese was ultimately fought out, not only by Greek and British commandos entering the islands in the waning days of the war, but by Dodecanesian-Americans as well: shopkeepers, tradesmen, and professionals in New York City. For the last chapter in the story we return to the scene of the beginning, to those groups of expatriated islanders banded together in an adopted land.

In 1939, assisted by donations, mostly from Kasiot shipowners recently arrived in New York, the Dodecanesian National Council was formed and moved to an office in Rockefeller Center. It hired secretaries and a clipping service, wrote letters to the press and members of the American government and put out a newspaper, *The Dodecanesian*.

In New York, the council sponsored a gala dinner to proclaim the *Enosis* of the Dodecanese with Greece. Though the announcement was premature, it was historically inevitable. The leaders of the movement were all expatriate islanders, and some of them had been born in *xenitia*. James Polychronis was born in Istanbul of parents from the island of Nisyros. Dr. Nicholas Mavris, a Kasiot and editor of *The Archive of Kasos* was born in Zaghazig in Egypt.

Later, when I was writing this book, Mr. Polychronis showed me a photograph of the dinner held in 1943 to celebrate the Italian surrender and to proclaim *Enosis* with Greece. The photograph was taken in a banquet room of the Hotel St. Moritz, which had become a meeting place of the Greek expatriate community. It showed several hundred Dodecanesians, assembled at tables according to the island of their origin.

At the head table I recognized the archbishop, Dr. Nicholas Mavris, and other directors of the council. And at a table among other Kasiots were Uncle George and Uncle Manuel, other relatives, and my mother and father. That night when my parents drove into New York City to this banquet of their ancestral island, I was left at home in my *xenitia*, by the golf course in Rye.

The bell-tower at Phry. Photo by Robert McCabe.

DEPARTURE

*T*he boat for Rhodes was scheduled to arrive at six in the morning, but a storm came up the day before and we weren't sure we could leave. The harbor at Kasos was too exposed, and if the wind persisted, the boat would stop in the open sea, blow its whistle, and go on to Rhodes without us. Either way, we wouldn't know until morning.

Our last night was an anxious one. With our bags packed, the plastic bags and shirt cardboards and rubber bands stuffed back into Uncle George's suitcase, we sat on the veranda and watched the sea. Across from us, the peaks of Karpathos faded in the distance. Below, darkness crept over the courtyard where my namesake had been married to Eleni Mavroleon, where a midwife had held up their first son, George, and where, to celebrate his christening, *mezitia* had been flung against the sky.

For the rest of the evening, villagers came to say good-bye. One old lady, who had a daughter living in America, came with a young man from the café, who carried a cardboard crate and set it down in front of us. She accepted a sweet of the spoon and a glass of water from Aphrodite. We looked at the crate while she talked, but she did not mention it. Then, after wishing us a good voyage several times, she told us she had a favor to ask.

"Will you take these *koulouria* to my daughter in Jackson Heights?" she said.

My uncle looked puzzled.

"But I am not going to America," said Uncle George. "I don't live there anymore."

"But your nephew does."

They looked at me.

"Ah, of course, my nephew can take them on his way home," said Uncle George.

I looked at Uncle George in amazement. Of course, in the hand I reserve for carrying bananas. I had come with bananas and could return with *koulouria*. As a fertility symbol, I had become hermaphroditic: eastward male, westward female.

I told the old lady I would take the *koulouria* to her daughter, and she blessed me and bade me a good journey.

After she had gone, I didn't have time to say anything to my uncle when an old gentleman appeared, carrying a large metal container. He too accepted a sweet of the spoon and wished us a good voyage, and he too had a favor to ask.

"Will you take these honeyfrittles to my cousin in New Jersey?" he said.

"Of course," said Uncle George. "My nephew will take them on his way home."

"Of course," I said.

The old man blessed me and bade us good-bye.

No more villagers came to pay their respects, and

for the rest of the evening we had to contend only with Aphrodite, who hovered around us, on imaginary errands.

"If you take that ship tomorrow, you'll drown for sure," she said. "And I won't weep for you. It'll serve you right, for bringing me back to this ruined island. In Alexandria, I had a house of my own and Arab servants to call me Kyra Aphrodite. And you brought me back and shut me up alone in this house, so I could end my days waiting for the roof to fall in upon my head.

"Came back to Kasos, did you? To my Eleni's house? And just as I said, you're ready to sail away again on the next ship. What do you want with Kasos, you and your nephews from England and America? Tomorrow you'll sail away, and I'll never see you again."

"We'll be back," said Uncle George. "We'll come back to see you."

"When? In another fifty years? I won't be here, and neither will the island. In fifty years, Kasos will be at the bottom of the sea, where it belongs. When you sail by on the ship to Rhodes, you'll see nothing but blue water. Anyway, I don't want you to come back. I was glad to see you, but I'm an old woman and I can't weep the way I used to. I don't want you to come here ever again, because I don't want to weep for you when you go."

With that, she went into the other house.

Uncle George and my cousin and I sat in silence. The peaks of Karpathos had vanished in the distance. Across the courtyard, in the farthest corner, we could see a lantern Aphrodite placed there to light the way to the toilet, burning like a votive light to Vasilios's lost archives.

The town was quiet. With forebodings of catastrophe in the air, of death by drowning and islands descending beneath the sea, Uncle George did not help dispel our mood. He remembered his last voyage as captain of his father's ship, when he was shipwrecked.

"What happened on that voyage, Uncle George?" I said, providing my usual cue.

"What happened? I'll tell you what. We were shipwrecked."

"Shipwrecked? And what do you remember about it?"

"I remember *dolmades*."

"*Dolmades?*"

"Wonderful *dolmades,* the sweetest I have ever eaten. They were made from vine-leaves grown near fresh water, by a spring near Port Said, and the fresh water made them exceptionally sweet."

"How did you happen to have these *dolmades* on that voyage when you were shipwrecked?"

"Not *dolmades*. One *dolma,*" he said. "I had one of them, and later the ship's whistle sounded and we all made for the lifeboats, and I nearly went on the long journey with the taste of that wonderful *dolma* in my mouth, and all the others lost forever."

Uncle George told the story of his shipwreck in 1916. It was his last voyage as captain of his father's steamship, returning to Greece from India. Afterwards, he retired from the sea to spend the rest of his life in shipping offices, first in London, then New York, and Piraeus.

His ship was named the *Lily,* a three-island steamship, so called because of its three islands:

fo'c'sle, bridge, and poop. He sailed her up the Red
Sea and through the Suez Canal. In Port Said he joined
a convoy, for in those dark days of 1916 the
Mediterranean was infested with submarines, and one
of them, *Port Said Jack,* terrorized ships sailing the
waters between Egypt and the Greek islands. For
every convoy that departed from Port Said, one ship
was sure to be sunk.

Jack struck only once, then vanished as suddenly
as he appeared, to elude any depth charges. Whenever
a convoy would set out, every captain wondered if his
ship had been chosen by the fates. The crews were
advised to keep their belongings packed and be ready
to abandon ship. And the British trawler, accompanying the convoy, made ready to pick up survivors.

"A relative gave me the *dolmades* in Port Said,"
said Uncle George. "Beautiful sweet *dolmades,* all
warm and steamy in a jar. I tasted one of them.
Delicious! And then Uncle John, my father's brother,
sailing with me, took the jar and put it where I
couldn't find it. I looked for it all day. That night *Port
Said Jack* struck us. Our ship went down and the *dolmades* with it."

"Was anybody lost?"

"No, only the *dolmades*. The trawler picked up
all hands. As soon as we were safe I asked Uncle John
what he had done with them. He said, 'I hid them so
you could have them for later.' *Have them for later?*
Well, he saw what happened, there wasn't any *later.*
I nearly went on the long journey with the taste of that
wonderful *dolma* in my mouth and the thought of all
the others to torment me for all eternity."

By now, I had decided I must make a deal with

Uncle George. I am so fastidious with hand luggage,
I must have been singled out for special torment: first
bananas, now honeyfrittles and a crateful of
koulouria.

"Make up your mind," I said, "it's either the
koulouria or the honey-frittles. One of them must stay."

And so we made a compromise, an accommoda-
tion between the two instincts descended in my family from Vasilios the saver and Old Yia-Yia the
disposer. We decided to take the honeyfrittles, which
were easier to carry, and left the *koulouria* in the
alcove off the living room, with the bananas. And
therein, in that fateful choice, lay the source of my
own catastrophe at sea.

In the morning the sea was calmer, though not
calm enough. The summer wind in the Aegean always
dies at night. But if there is wind in the early morning, as the day wears on there is sure to be a storm.
At five, the ship was sighted, turning stubbornly in the
uneasy sea.

The peaks of Karpathos were just showing
through the morning mist. Above the highest of them
hung a white cloud: an ominous portent.

"In two hours, you'll be drowned," said
Aphrodite, risen in her spotted bathrobe, the white
kerchief around her head. "Tonight we'll be singing
dirges for you."

The car arrived at the end of the row of balconies.
After loading, we turned back to say good-bye to
Aphrodite. She was standing at the gate. Before her,
the three of us stood sheepishly, like children.

"Go," she said. "Go quickly."

We said good-bye.

"Yes, good-bye," she said. "Good-bye to George, to the two Eliases. Good-bye to Aphrodite."

We left her where we found her, by a blue door in a wall of white, standing watch over an empty house.

The ship's whistle sounded. It had emerged full-blown, advancing steadily toward the harbor.

The car rattled through the empty streets, past the placid pool of the Bucca, past the bell tower with the clock. The town was asleep, colorless in the hour before the sunrise.

We boarded without ceremony, and as the ship slipped out of that unattended harbor at six o'clock, exactly on schedule, Kasos was behind us.

A few minutes later, as soon as we were clear, the wind came up and the ship began to roll. In the open water, the sea became a field of demons. The ship plunged one way and then another. Very soon, I felt as sick as any rabbi.

"A storm after all," I said to Uncle George.

"A good one," he said.

I sat with my face buried in my sleeve, while Uncle George narrated to the wind.

"Later, Uncle," I said. "Later, please."

I thought we would never make it to Karpathos. There were moments I wanted to jump overboard, to put an end to my misery. I had to keep perfectly still, eyes closed and face covered, to avoid the slightest movement. Even to listen to Uncle George or look around me was too much.

"*Koulouria* are very good for that," said Uncle.

"For what?"

"For what you are feeling now . . . for sea-sickness."

I remembered once on an earlier summer, I was in a storm off Syros, and when I thought I was going to be sick, someone gave me a *koulouri* to chew and I felt marvelously better. The dough of the *koulouri* is so dry and hard that it absorbs all the rancors of the stomach, and Greek sailors use it instead of dramamine.

Then I saw my error. I had left behind all those marvelous *koulouria*, which would have worked my cure, and in their place I had honeyfrittles, sticky sweet and sickly. So, like Uncle George, I was tormented with imaginings: a gross of Kasiot *koulouria,* rare therapeutic delicacies, abandoned forever on the island.

Two hours later, when the ship sailed into the lee of Karpathos and the wind subsided, when I looked around at last, Kasos was gone.

Some weeks later I was in New York. Uncle George had returned to his office in Piraeus for another winter. I had left him the tape recorder, and on my side of the Atlantic I got another one. Now, instead of filling long pages with his tiny hand, Uncle George had only to summon the genie, turn him on, and speak.

By that time I had begun this book, and as the earlier chapters were completed, I sent them to Uncle George and asked for his comments. I wondered how he would take to the new medium. Would he be comfortable before a microphone, speaking into a genie's indifferent ear?

When the first tape arrived, I didn't wonder any-more. Ever since dictaphones were invented, Uncle George had used them passionately. I used to see him in the office in New York, sitting among several con-versations going on around him, mumbling endless monologues into a metal ear. Now he spoke to me across the ocean exactly as though dictating a busi-ness letter.

"My dear Elias," he said, "*comma*. I received your letter today asking for my thoughts on the chap-ters which you sent me *period*. I hope you will agree that it would not be proper for me personally to dare to make corrections, but reading your book, I see that certain facts have been completely changed, for exam-ple in the chapter entitled 'The Way to Phry.'"

As he became involved in what he was saying, he forgot to specify the punctuation. After a while, out of a tape recorder whose silent rotations made circu-lar reflections on my ceiling, Uncle George talked to me from his office in Piraeus. Every so often, behind his desk, I could hear the shutter rattling in the har-bor wind.

"Perhaps it was my fault in not having described everything carefully," he said. "For this purpose, I will repeat the story of our return from Syros and my par-ents' departure for Egypt, exactly as I remember it."

Another Way to Phry, I thought. I had put on the tape at about midnight; at two o'clock, Uncle George was still talking.

"The *Anastasia*, you remember, was in Syros with a cargo of roof tiles, chartered at five francs a ton. 'What do you expect to do with five francs a ton?' my father's brother Nicholas asked him. As you have stated in the book, we used to tease Mavrandonis, floating his hat in the soapy water. And mind you, he was the terror of the sailors.

"They were very good sailors, and often they finished their work very quickly, and he had nothing more to give them. In those days, we kept a hog on board. Whenever the sailors finished their work ahead of time, Mavrandonis would tell them, 'Go and bring the hog on deck. Poor creature, he needs some air.'

"Then, the next day, if they finished their work again, he would say, 'Take the hog below. Poor creature, it will die of cold.' The sailors grumbled, 'Up with the hog, down with the hog.' And that became a proverb among us, for any sort of futile labor.

"Even now, I often tell my wife, when she constantly rearranges the furniture in our living room, 'Up with the hog, down with the hog.'

"When peace was declared, my father prepared to deliver the roof tiles to Russia, and then go on to Alexandria with my mother, taking baby Nicholas and the nurse with them. Basil and I were sent home to Kasos in a caïque, not in the *Anastasia*.

"On our way back in the caïque, I remember stopping at the island of Astakia, which belongs to Kasos: a small rocky island where we found a pool of rainwater and filled one or two casks to enable us to continue on to Kasos. Two of the crew brought out fishing lines, because in the crystal clear water, we could see some pretty large fish playing at the bottom."

So what I have written is wrong. The *Anastasia* did not anchor in the lee of Makra Island, and the caique did not go out to meet her. Eleni and her two boys did not ply that windy passage, and the boys did not hold the gunwales like brave cavaliers, riding the white horses home to Phry.

As the truth is revealed, it reveals the mischief of the mind. The mistake occurred between Uncle George and me. I never asked how he returned to Kasos, only assumed it was on the *Anastasia*.

So after circling the island, we could go around it once again. As the plastic spool dispenses Uncle George's voice, it spins another Kasos. On this second turning, the light hits Kasos from a different angle, and we see aspects of the island we missed before.

We see the island of Astakia, north of Kasos and west of Karpathos, where Kasiot shepherds used to take their flocks to graze. We see Mavrandonis's hog, the bane of *Anastasia's* crew, preserved in proverb long after his demise so that it roots on, incongruously, in Uncle George's living room. We see a spring, with crystal clear water, and fish chasing each other around the bottom.

In this way the journey will never be over. Aphrodite's gloomy augury may come true: with the passage of time Kasos will slip back into the sea; but that would make no difference. Kasos does not lie between Crete and Karpathos, except in reality.

Because there is no arrival or departure for us, no beginning and no journey's end, because we are doomed to sail the sea interminably between the past and future, I can leave the journey only in a way station.

From Rhodes, Uncle George and I returned to Athens. Some days later we went to spend the afternoon with an old Kasiot woman who lived an hour outside of town. She was over ninety, but in good health and in perfect possession of her memory. Like

my old aunts in Syros, she had come from Kasos years
before and was living out her *xenitia* in an Athenian
suburb.

Her son was a shipowner who lived in London,
(Anthony Papadakis, the father of twin boys Nicky
and George who were my playmates in Westchester
in the 1940s) but she preferred the hills of Attica,
where her daughter took care of her. She had not seen
my uncle in many years, but she greeted him as
though he visited her the week before. He introduced
me in the usual Kasiot mode, as Elias of Michael. But
either this statement of my lineage did not mean much
to her, or she felt my age disqualified me from any
communication; for she did not speak to me.

We were shown into the dining room. The old
woman sat in the corner in her black dress and cowl,
with Uncle George beside her. I sat some distance
away, across a table. On the wall above the woman's
head, I saw a tinted photo of her son, in a business
suit and an austere pose appropriate to the City of
London.

Outside, sprinklers cooled the lawn on a burning
August afternoon. The shutters were all closed
against the heat, and inside, with its stone floor and
wooden furniture without upholstery, the room was
cool and dark.

The old woman and Uncle George began to talk,
and soon they did not seem aware of my presence. I
spread my arms on the table, rested my chin on my
hands, and watched them.

I realized that whenever one comes upon certain
scenes of childhood, one feels exactly the way one did
as a child. Now, listening to Uncle George and the old

woman, I felt as I had in childhood, overhearing one of those ancient, unintelligible conversations in my house in Rye. I felt as I had before, perhaps accompanying my father on some unfathomable errand, waiting to get on to some business that I could understand. As I listened, for a moment I heard the liquid polysyllables that had once been so bewildering, Romaic echoes of the past.

But now I could understand them. The syllables composed a language.

Still, the others did not observe me. Still, they ignored me perfectly. As I sat in the accustomed attitude of childhood, chin on my hands, I felt as I had before, too young to know what they were talking about, too ignorant even to ask a question. I didn't make a sound, only turned my uncomprehending face toward them, my understanding hidden behind it as completely as the tape recorder had been hidden beneath the table.

The old woman was telling about the customs of the island, about the custom of *proxenia* and *emvasmata*, of naming children, of wailing dirges for the dead. She told about a feast known as Kleithona, about a certain doctor who couldn't decide which of two girls to marry, about a vengeance.

That was the final surprise. I knew the stories they were telling. I'd heard them all before. As I sat with my chin cradled in my open palms, I knew at last, if I could have had any doubt, that childhood was over. There were no unknown stories for me, no more mysterious words.

But unaware of this, not seeing the silent face across the table, the old woman turned to Uncle George.

"By the way, George," she said. "My grandson told me a shocking thing. He mentioned the story of your great-grandmother, Hazimanolis' widow, and he said you told him the widow wanted Basil Kikos dead because she'd slept with him, once when Hazimanolis was away at sea, and she took that opportunity to have him killed and bury her shame."

Uncle George was astounded. Even I, across the table, blinked. Just as I predicted, one of the cats was back: a monstrous, deformed copy of the original. But, ironically, it was one my uncle had not engendered.

"Impossible," said Uncle George. "I could not have said that because it isn't true."

"Are you sure?"

"Of course. How could I have said it? I heard the story from many different people and I never heard that from anyone. The widow wanted Basil Kikos dead because his death must pay for her husband's death. An eye for an eye, a life for a life."

"I believe you, George," the old woman said. "My grandson must have got it wrong somehow. Or he just made it up to tease me."

She paused a moment, peering to the limits of her shuttered world. Then, still seeing only George, still not perceiving the stranger from another world, his own demon making silent circles in his head, she told my uncle: "But it makes me think, George, from now on we'd better keep these stories to ourselves. Maybe we'd better not talk about the past so much, at least when the young people are around."

ABOUT THE AUTHOR

*E*lias B. Kulukundis was born in London, journeyed to Greece when he was one (on the Orient Express) and came to America when he was three. Nevertheless, he feels that he grew up in a Greek world.

After graduating from the Phillips Exeter Academy and Harvard, he learned Russian and translated *Both Sides of the Ocean* by the Soviet novelist Viktor Nekrasov. He then turned his western education to uncovering his Greek roots, and as he says, started reading about Greece as though it were France or England, beginning in the present and working backwards.

A hybrid product himself, Kulukundis feels at home in the Greek universe, whether around a sophisticated dinner table of Greek exiles in London or New York, or delving into the darker motivations of the Aegean islands.

Once a shipping financier as well as a writer, he now spends most of his time writing and his leisure time singing musical comedy and opera.

He has combined these interests in his latest work,

a libretto for a musical entitled "Three Brides For Kasos," to be produced in Canada summer of 2005.

He has raised a daughter, Delia, who is a graduate of Swarthmore College.

He lives in New York City.